AIMS

AIMS

*A Brief Metaphysics
for Today*

James W. Felt

University of Notre Dame Press

Notre Dame, Indiana

Designed by Wendy McMillen
Set in 10.1/13.6 Sabon by Four Star Books

Library of Congress Cataloging-in-Publication Data

Felt, James W., 1926–
Aims : a brief metaphysics for today / James W. Felt.
    p.   cm.
Includes bibliographical references and index.
ISBN-13: 978-0-268-02901-2 (pbk. : alk. paper)
ISBN-10: 0-268-02901-6 (pbk. : alk. paper)
1. Metaphysics.   I. Title.
BD111. F275   2007
110—dc22

                                2007030482

∞ *This paper meets the requirements of ANSI/NISO Z39.48-1992 (Permanence of Paper).*

For Richard and Rosemary Blackwell

Contents

AIMS

—

Preface

"Know yourself!" challenged the Oracle of Delphi, and philosophers engaged in *metaphysics* or "first philosophy" have struggled to meet that challenge ever since. No ordinary kind of knowing, metaphysics necessarily includes knowing our relation to the peopled world in which we live. Neither is it scientific knowing in the modern sense. It is such an unusual kind of knowing that its peculiarity has led many modern philosophers to deny that it exists or could even make any sense.

I disagree with that view and submit the following short essay as a project in metaphysics. Now no philosophic view, even if it is internally coherent, is directly demonstrable. It can only recommend itself as more consonant with and illuminative of direct human experience than its denial.

As illustrative of what I mean by metaphysical knowing, I cite this description of it by Etienne Gilson: "Metaphysics is *the knowledge gathered by a naturally transcendent reason in its search for the first principles, or first causes, of what is given in sensible experience.*"[1] There are two peripheral points implied in this description.

The first point is the question of how we derive the principles underlying such an account in terms of causes and principles. In this regard I submit that we normally adopt such principles to the degree that they seem consonant with what we find in immediate experience, as well as illuminative of that experience when taken in their full-blown applications. There is no getting away from looking at the world through some set of philosophic assumptions or other, but the adoption of such assumptions is more often subconscious and implicit than recognized, and implicit assumptions are all the more influential for their being unnoticed.

The second point is that such a set of principles, acknowledged or implied, constitutes a *metaphysical perspective* that in turn establishes a possible *intelligible horizon* determinative of the sort of objective world that can be recognized from such a perspective. As Oz explained to Dorothy, everything in Emerald City looked green to her because she was wearing green glasses. The world revealed to us in our philosophy is pretty much the world we were looking for, the world that fits our adopted philosophic perspective.

The aim of this essay is to establish just such a philosophic perspective through which we can plausibly view ourselves and our relation to the world. In short it is to respond, at least in a limited and provisional way, to the Delphic challenge. The result will be a brief, bare-bones metaphysics, but a metaphysics nonetheless.

It may be helpful to the reader to know the provenance of this essay. In the early 1970s I proposed that it might be worth trying to combine the better insights and principles of the philosophies of St. Thomas Aquinas of the thirteenth century and Alfred North Whitehead of the twentieth, while omitting what seem to be the weaker aspects, so as to achieve a transformed and more modern philosophic perspective.[2] In my book *Coming To Be* (2001) I very belatedly published a defense and first sketch of what such a metaphysics might be like. The present essay is the natural follow-up of this project, but here I pay much less attention to the actual philosophies of Aquinas and Whitehead and much more to my own manner of melding the two. I leave it to the reader to judge whether the attempt is successful, at least as a beginning.

Of course there are other philosophic influences at work here as well, and I want to acknowledge that the chief intellectual assumptions dominating the following discussion seem to me to be the following:

(1) The ontology of St. Thomas Aquinas whose central philosophic insight pivots around participation in the act of existing (*esse*) with its bipolar directionality reminiscent of Plotinus: its flowing from a Source and its simultaneous orientation back toward that Source.

(2) Henri Bergson's stress on the intuitive aspect of philosophic insight, of the distinction between the continuity inherent in immediate experience and that of quantity or space, and of the authenticity of the feeling of freedom within human deciding.

(3) Alfred North Whitehead's recognition of a level of sensory experience that runs deeper than what is ordinarily noticed. On this more fundamental level we are immediately aware of being causally influenced by things in the world, of the derivation of the present from the past, and of the value dimension of experience that partially grounds a teleological metaphysics.

(4) The phenomenological point of view, such as that of Maurice Merleau-Ponty, with its subject-object polarity of experience and its perspectival-horizonal view of the world.[3]

In the considerations that follow I have allowed the argument to grow by itself in a natural way. Thus the elaboration is self-referential, sometimes repetitious, and cumulative rather than linear (which would be far from natural). For that reason I venture to make the same appeal as did George Berkeley in the preface to his *Treatise Concerning the Principles of Human Knowledge*: that the reader withhold judgment on this view until he or she has read through the whole with the attention it may seem to deserve.[4]

Whatever the merit of this present experiment in constructive metaphysics, I wish to express indebtedness to my philosophy teachers and colleagues over many years whose wisdom has doubtless affected my thinking in more ways than I know. I think especially of W. Norris Clarke, S.J., of Fordham University, and of John H. Wright, S.J., of Gonzaga University, who opened for me the riches of the philosophic thought of St. Thomas Aquinas; of Richard J. Blackwell and the late Leonard J. Eslick, model philosophers and teachers at Saint Louis University; and of Lewis S. Ford of Old Dominion University who has for all these years benevolently challenged me with the thought of Alfred North Whitehead. I am grateful to Santa Clara University for a Presidential Research Grant in the spring of 2002 that gave the initial impetus to this essay, and to my sister for helping to make the writing possible.

J. W. F.

Chapter 1

The Beginning

1.1 THE BEGINNING IS EXPERIENCING

That is where we find ourselves and the world, so there is no other place from which to start a philosophic analysis. But I do not mean by "experiencing" what has been fashionable since Descartes' disastrous experiment in mind-body dualism. I do not presuppose that experiencing is purely mental. I accept it for what it purports to be, an activity that relates me as a bodily subject to a surrounding objective world of which I am myself a part. The goal of a metaphysical analysis of experience is to uncover the intelligible richness of this relationship.

The natural first stage in forming such an analysis consists in trying to notice the most philosophically significant aspects of that act of experiencing. That is an exercise in phenomenological description. Such a description can profit from some of the more recent advances in science and in philosophic awareness, particularly the twentieth century's attention to dynamic activity or process.

The second stage consists in attempting to make experience, so described, intelligible in terms of a coherent framework of philosophic concepts. A genuine metaphysical account of experience adds the dimension of intelligibility and thereby enriches that same experience. Compare it to astronomers' understanding of a star-filled desert night. We can all gaze at the same points of light, but astronomers see them from the perspective of a coherent theoretical understanding that enriches their experience by giving it deeper intelligible meaning. And indeed, it seems safe to say that astronomers' chief goal is not the hope of ultimately building better air conditioners but the sheer satisfaction of better understanding the cosmos in which we all live. In somewhat the same way philosophers aim to reach a more satisfying intellectual grasp of our experienced world.[1] Now, multifarious experience, like any multiplicity, can be satisfactorily understood only in terms of some single, underlying pattern discovered within it. The metaphysician is in search of such a pattern.

The third and final stage of the philosophic excursion we are about to undertake will be to return once more to experience itself and notice whether, or to what extent, the proposed philosophic framework illuminates and enriches that experience. In particular, we shall in the end note the relevance of the system to several classic philosophic problems, such as the grounds for an ethics and an aesthetics, the existence and nature of human freedom, whether there exists a unique entity that fits at least some of the notions historically attributed to God, and what might be the possibilities for individual human destiny.

1.2 HUMAN EXPERIENCING REVEALS THE STRUCTURE OF NATURAL ACTIVITY

Natural activity is the ongoing process of becoming in the world. In attempting to uncover the intelligible structure of human experiencing I am deliberately assuming what at first may sound outlandish, namely, that the basic structure of human experience reflects the most fundamental structure of all natural activity. This assumption is not new. Henri Bergson, for instance, wrote: "The matter and life which fill the world are equally within us; the forces which work in all things we feel within ourselves; whatever may be the inner essence of what is and what is done, we are of that essence."[2] Alfred North Whitehead echoes this, less lyrically but just as deliberately: "In describing the capacities, realized or unrealized, of an actual occasion [Whitehead's term for an ontological unit of experiencing], we have, with Locke, tacitly taken human experience as an example upon which to found the generalized description required for metaphysics. But when we turn to the lower organisms we have first to determine which among such capacities fade from realization into irrelevance, that is to say, by comparison with human experience which is our standard."[3]

That immediate experience should reveal the structure of cosmic becoming is, after all, only to be expected unless we are to suppose that we human beings are extrinsic to the evolutionary universe, somehow pasted onto it rather than emerging from it. Today we are increasingly aware that, despite the general trend in the cosmos toward an increase of disorder on the large scale, there is nevertheless also a counterthrust toward the order required by life, sentience, and intelligence. Human consciousness is the present peak of this cosmic evolution toward finer activities, and so it is reasonable to think that this same consciousness, in its ability to reflect upon itself, should discover within itself the basic structure of cosmic process generally. Human consciousness is a privileged perspective from which to view the world, so that metaphysical reflection upon experience reveals something about the world as much as about ourselves.[4]

This supposition fits the presumption of a certain version of realism about sensation that pervades the following discussion. By that I mean the well-founded presumption that in and through our experiencing we encounter an objective, extramental world of which we are a part. I shall claim that the world gives itself to us in the act of sense perception. If that is the case, then metaphysical reflection upon our experience is not a purely subjective, psychological exercise but also a reflection of the given world.

Unfortunately such a theory of perception has been mainly out of style for three and a half centuries. Because of a series of philosophic mistakes, the dominant epistemological viewpoint has been a kind of deformed idealism that is fairly called representational. Let me briefly sketch how it goes, so as to set it into clear contrast with the view that I shall be holding in the rest of this essay.

1.3 THE REPRESENTATIONAL THEORY OF PERCEPTION

From our earliest childhood we took for granted, I think, that our sensations put us in touch with a world around us full of rocks and trees, birds and people. Only later in life did we run into philosophic arguments that claimed to show that in sense perceiving we don't directly encounter objects in an external world at all but rather sensations in our own minds that we then, by inference, interpret as representing the extramental objects that presumably provoked the sensations.

The arguments seemed airtight. The car that looked teal green in sunlight looked gray under the lights of a parking lot. The appearance of the car had undeniably changed, yet the car itself presumably had not. It thus seemed to follow that the appearance we observed was in our minds rather than a physical reality in the world. Similar cases, involving any of our other external senses, can be multiplied indefinitely. The conclusion seems to be that in sensing we are given only appearances in our mind, but that we take them to represent the objects outside the mind, which we suppose provoked those appearances in us. Hence the distinction, almost standard in philosophy ever since Descartes and Locke, between (mental) appearance and (material) reality, with its inbuilt problem of how the two realms, mind and matter, could possibly relate to each other. It is not too much to say that philosophy in the Western world has for 350 years struggled, mostly unsuccessfully, to get the perceiver out of his or her mind and into an external world. For according to this accepted theory, our perceiving finds us inside a mental world of appearances, and we get to a physical world, if we do it at all, only by a secondhand process of questionable inference.

But where does this theory, at first so plausible, go wrong? For one thing it incorrectly assumes, explicitly or implicitly, that in the act of perceiving we are given either external objects as they are in themselves or else our own perceptions (variously called sense data, sensa, sense impressions, sensations, or appearances). Now it is easy to rule out objects themselves because what we experience in perception—the appearances—varies even when we think that the objects themselves do not. If, then, we must choose between mental appearances and external objects as the immediate objects of perceiving, we have to pick the former. We have to conclude that in sensing we are confronted only with appearances in our minds, not with external objects.

1.4 RELATIONAL REALISM

But we don't have to live with this theory. We don't have to think that we perceive either a mental representation of a world or objects just as they are in themselves. We can adopt a view of relational realism that affirms that in perceiving we do encounter real extramental objects, yet not objects in themselves but objects as they stand related to us in the act of perceiving.[5] In that way I reject the dichotomy that underlies representationalism: that we perceive either things-in-themselves or else sensations in the mind. Instead, I introduce, as it were in between the two, yet a third alternative: relational things, or things in relation to the perceiver.

In perceiving we do indeed sense real bodies in the world: not bodies as they exist in themselves, however, but bodies as they relate to us in the act of perceiving—that is, relational bodies. The seen-car (the perceptually related car) was really green in the sunlight because the sunlight itself made the car visible to me as green. The same car was really gray under artificial light for a similar reason. Innumerable factors enter into a single act of perception, and they all play a part in the relationality of the perceived object.

Besides rejecting the (mental) appearance versus (material) reality dichotomy of representationalism, relational realism depends upon accepting a richer theory of causality than is recognized in representationalism. The latter theory is infected with the isolationist view of causality of David Hume. Hume decreed—by what William James would call a Machtspruch— that every event must be just itself, bearing no internal connections to any other event. Consequently the events we call cause and effect are quite distinct from each other, so that it is impossible to argue from one to the other.

But that too is a mistake, just as is the false dichotomy of appearance versus reality. One can, justifiably to experience, accept the wisdom of Aristotle's insight that the activity of the cause is in its effect. Thus the car itself is acting on me, through the light and the consequent immutation of my retinas. I thus see the car in its acting on me rather than merely a mental representation of the car.[6]

1.5 RELATIONAL REALISM AND COSMIC PROCESS

Relational realism naturally invites assumption 1.2 above: that conscious reflection on what is happening in our own sensing may reveal to us the anatomy of cosmic process in general, not just of sensing. For if the true objects of sensing are not mental appearances but the world as related to us in sensing, it makes sense to suppose that sensing gives us an opening into the workings of the cosmos. With that in mind, let us attempt a more detailed description of the world as given to us in perception and of the general structure of perceiving itself.

Chapter 2

A Brief Description
of Experiencing

Trying to notice the character of your own act of perceiving is a little like trying to notice what your eyeglass lenses are like while you are wearing them. Sense experiencing is aimed at the things of the world around us, not at itself; its own character is not an object of our experience. So let us begin by asking what experiencing seems to reveal to us about those extramental objects themselves. Later we shall further inquire into the structure of experiencing itself.

2.1 EXPERIENCING EXTRAMENTAL OBJECTS

In our sensing we seem to find ourselves face to face with external bodies of all sorts that present themselves to us. But on closer examination we notice that bodies not only present themselves, we sense them as acting upon us in provoking the sensing itself. Here we are at a level of sensing that runs deeper than appearances such as colors, shapes, and smells. The sun that wakes us in the morning, the slamming door, are *felt as affecting us,* as impacting us whether we like it or not.[1]

Though this feeling of being acted upon by extramental objects seems a plain fact of experience, most philosophers, following David Hume, have denied its objective authenticity. But Hume's argument is unsound: he entertained too narrow a conception of what a "sense impression" could amount to, and he looked for the experience of causal influence in the wrong places. He was right in denying that we have any sense impression of the causal influence of one billiard ball on another, but wrong in overlooking the influence of things in the world on *himself*. If a billiard ball had been bounced off his forehead, would he have *felt affected* by it? (Skeptical readers may try the experiment for themselves.) I therefore deny Hume's denial and accept as authentic the feeling within sense perception of being confronted with, because influenced by, external, though relational, objects. It is perfectly reasonable to suppose that sense experiencing is what it seems to be: an *encounter with extramental objects that affect us.*

2.2 DERIVATION AND THE WORLD

Fused with this feeling of causal influence is the feeling of the present *deriving from* the past and of the future emerging from the present. It is the feeling both of the *continuity of experience* and of the world thus encountered. It is a feeling of the continuity through time of the experienced world.

I have repeatedly spoken of a *world*. For the objects of our perception do not give themselves to us singly but rather as *constituting a whole,* a world, of which we feel we are ourselves a part even though there is simultaneously an inescapable feeling of *otherness* in their self-manifestation. They are other than us, yet form a whole of which we are a part. In our sensing we both feel a world and feel ourselves part of it.

2.3 THE FEELING OF VALUE

Included in our feeling of the external world is the *feeling of value or worth,* good or bad, a feeling of its *importance.* The world does not present itself to us in experience as irrelevant or making no difference. It comes freighted with a dimension of good or bad, of desirability or peril.

A simple but clear example of what I mean is the experience of seeing colors. We treasure the sense world in its colors far more than if we had to experience it only in shades of gray. There is no demonstrating this assertion; we have only to look at a red rose to recognize its truth, and I apologize to any readers who happen to be color-blind. Is there any amount of money you would accept in return for seeing the world thereafter only in shades of gray?

Now according to the usual viewpoint, the colors we sense are in themselves value-neutral, but we then subjectively attach more or less value to them according to our tastes. What I am claiming here, however, in agreement with Whitehead, is that the *feeling of worth* forms part of the original experience of seeing the color. We *find* value in color vision because we experience it, we do not make it up afterward. This holds true even though it is possible for us deliberately to increase our own sensitivity to the enjoyment of color vision.

2.4 REACTING TO THE WORLD

The above observations on immediate experience provide a natural framework for another of its characters, which is its *stimulus-response* dynamic. The experienced world is felt as both making a difference to us and as calling for an appropriate response. That "difference" takes many forms: of influence on body or mind, of delight or danger, of possibilities for good or bad. And the response called for is—sometimes, at least—

a free decision on our part. By its experienced impact on us, the circumambient world every moment calls on us to respond to it. The story of our lives is woven onto the ongoing succession of such responses.

Whitehead has pointed out that these responses or decisions have a *synthetic* character. That is, they can be regarded as fusing all the welter of immediately past fact and possibility into a new, unified whole. The decision amounts to dismissing countless conceived possibilities in favor of one emergent, coherent actuality.

2.5 THE FEELING OF AIM

We also find that in our deliberate experiencing—as distinguished from indeliberate or purely automatic reactions, such as sneezing—we are always *aiming at some goal,* at achieving some new good. Aristotle pointed out that we ultimately seek happiness in every deliberate choice. This aim at some not-yet-attained good provides both the spur for deliberate action and the form that that action will take. Deliberate human action is *teleological,* goal-aimed.

2.6 OUR SELVES AS SUBJECTS

In the above reflections lurks, tacitly taken for granted, the most important of all the characteristics of immediate experience, at least of sensible experience: that *it gives itself as the act of a subject (of experiencing) involved with an objective world.* Sensible experience is inescapably *bipolar,* embodying a dynamic relationship between the objects experienced and the experiencer. There is necessarily both a for-me-ness and a by-me-ness in sensing. The world and its objects give themselves to me in sensing and the sensing is itself my response. Also, *I* experience the present, not only of the world but of experience itself, as deriving from the past, and the future from the present. In its subjective aspect this is nothing other than my sense of *self-identity through time* even through internal changes. Also, the value or importance felt in immediate experience is always a value *for me,* and the challenge of the immediate past to take account of it is always a challenge *to me* as to the subject called upon to act. The synthetic decision that is the essence of experience is a decision that *I* must make, and *I* aim at satisfaction in my deliberate actions.

I call this subject-object relationship within experiencing *bipolar* by analogy with the poles of a bar magnet. The field of the magnet can be understood as a dynamic relationship between the two poles, neither of which can exist on its own but both of which are necessary for the field. The act of sensibly experiencing the world is a little like that.

Of course I, who am a subject experiencing, am aware of myself experiencing in quite a different way than I am of the objects toward which experience is normally directed. I never encounter my very self in my experiencing in the same way that I encounter objects in the world. I, as acting subject, am always present within my experiencing but never as an experienced object.

A camera furnishes a useful analogy here. There is a clear sense in which a camera, by its construction and purpose, never takes a picture of itself (mirrors possibly excepted). Yet there is an obvious sense in which the camera is *present* in all its pictures, though never as an object. The capabilities or flaws of the camera permeate every picture it takes, so that a professional photographer could tell you a lot about the camera just by examining a number of its pictures.

Even otherwise astute philosophers have sometimes failed to notice the nonobjective but very real presence of the subject in the act of experiencing. A notorious case is found in David Hume's *Treatise of Human Nature.* He writes: "When I enter most intimately into what I call *myself,* I always stumble on some particular perception or other, of heat or cold, light or shade, love or hatred, pain or pleasure. I never can catch *myself* at any time without a perception, and never can observe any thing but the perception."[2] But Hume fails to find him*self* in his experiencing because he is looking for himself as an object instead of as a subject. He writes: "*I* enter . . . *I* stumble . . . *I* never can catch myself." But who is this self whom Hume is looking for and always fails to find in his searching? Who, please, is doing the searching if not the very self that is sought? The searcher is not an object-I but a subject-I, an experiencing-I rather than an (objectively) experienced-I. It is the agent-I that inhabits experience and for whom other things are objects.

2.7 INTERACTIVITY AND PERSONAL RELATIONS

The subject-object polarity of experiencing is not only the natural structure or form of experiencing, it is a dynamic relationship constituted by *interactivity*. I find myself in a world of which I am myself a part. I know this because I experience the activity of the things in the world upon me, and I am called upon to respond creatively to this world by my own activity. In a word, the activity of experiencing is an interactivity. Experiencing is never isolated, never detached and wrapped up exclusively in itself. Descartes notwithstanding, there can never be a finite instance of something that needs nothing else in order to exist. The least observation of the results of modern science confirms the universality of this experience of interactivity, from the pervasive power of gravitational and electromagnetic fields to the interconnection of biological events that ground ecology.

There is, however, one form of this interactive relationship that stands out as unique. This is the experience of interpersonal relations, of dealing with other subjects of experiencing, of dealing with other I's. This is commonly referred to as the problem of intersubjectivity. That it should be a problem is curious, since nothing is more concrete and basic within our experience than our awareness that in very many of our activities we are dealing with other persons.

But for someone holding a representational theory of perception, such an admission would scarcely be possible because it would be necessary to try to piece together other persons by a series of inferences: from sense data to presumed extramental physical causes of the data, and then from the physical causes to mentality. But in holding an epistemology of relational realism I can accept the conviction of Whitehead, who, when asked about the problem of how we know minds other than our own, exclaimed: "Hang it all! *Here we are. We don't go behind that, we begin with it!"*[3]

I propose that the above observations about the character of immediate experiencing are at least approximately correct and deserving of rational explication in terms of a system of metaphysical concepts. But before beginning this analysis, we require a clearer conception of how to proceed and of the necessary structure of any such analysis.

Chapter 3

Interlude on Method

3.1 PERSPECTIVES AND HORIZONS

Every act of understanding, including this attempted metaphysical analysis of immediate experience, is inevitably *perspectival*. For all forms of knowledge are perspectival. Here is what I mean.

I say "perspectival" by analogy with visual perception. Everything we see, we see from a particular standpoint or perspective. If there be a perspectiveless view of anything, we haven't got it and can't even imagine what it would be like. Furthermore, the perspective from which anything can be viewed naturally defines a "horizon" of all possible objects that can be seen from that perspective. The crow's nest on a ship provides a wider and more distant horizon than is available from the bridge. Perspective and horizon are linked polarities within vision.

If we stretch the analogy, perspective can also refer to the visual capacities of the viewer. Even within the band of electromagnetic energy within which human vision takes place, some people see more sharply than others. It is also established that some animals or insects see within a somewhat different band of the light-energy spectrum than we do. They can be said to see from a different perspective that defines for them a different horizon of possible objects of their vision.

The analogy takes on still more interest when applied to the set of *expectations or preconceptions* that inevitably color our intellectual understanding of any situation. Even in our vision we tend to see what we were expecting to see. All the more is this true with regard to the preconceptions that underlie understanding. We tend to understand situations from the perspective of the preconceptions that we bring to the experience. Perhaps that is why one seldom wins an argument concerning religion or politics.

Here is an illustration of the relation between perspective and horizon. Suppose that three persons are standing side by side viewing a landscape. The first is a military commander, the second a real estate developer, the third an artist. I think there is a clear sense in which, although they all are *looking at* the same valley, each one *sees* a different valley from what the others see. One sees a possible avenue for attack or defense; another sees a site for profitable construction; the third sees a configuration of colors and forms. What they *see* is *experiential* and is a function of the intentional perspectives they bring to the experience. None *sees* a valley-in-itself because none experiences a valley-in-itself. But the experienced, *seen* valley is different for each, according to the difference of their respective perspectives, even though the same *looked-at* (not experienced) valley is causally operative in each experience.

The same is true of any theoretic understanding of what is given in experience. Were I competent to do so, I could elect to analyze the characteristics of experience described in the previous chapter purely from the standpoint of electrochemical brain reactions. In so doing I could understand a good deal about them but only from that limited perspective, for the choice of that conceptual perspective automatically limits the horizon of intelligibility to the electrochemical domain. It provides no information as to whether or not other domains of understanding are available for fathoming experience.

The horizon or field for understanding, then, is determined by the conceptual perspectives that we bring to the analysis. These perspectives are chiefly embodied in the philosophic principles that we adopt for the sake of understanding. Some of these principles are only implicit and taken for granted, the result of temperament and social conditioning, but all the more powerful for being hidden. Others are deliberately chosen.

3.2 SENSE PERCEPTION IS PERSPECTIVAL

By now it is clear that sense perception, as we described it in chapter 2, is itself through and through perspectival. The acuity of our sense organs, the sort of medium available (for instance, the kind of light), and our physical situation with respect to the object, constitute together a particular perspective from or through which we sense the object. The appearing object, as thoroughly relational, embodies all these factors.[1] This is just to say that it belongs to the horizon of sensibility governed by that perspective.

3.3 ON CHOOSING A METAPHYSICAL PERSPECTIVE

Besides defining a horizon for understanding, philosophic principles bear within themselves certain consequential necessities that reach beyond the understanding of any immediate actuality. They define what it is still possible to think. As one philosopher put it: "Philosophers are free to lay down their own sets of principles, but once this is done, they no longer think as they wish—they think as they can."[2] Or as Aldous Huxley put it: "You pays your money and you takes your choice."[3]

If philosophers are indeed free to choose their own principles, what criteria can they use for selecting them? Surely not compatibility with more fundamental principles, since the principles here in question are themselves supposed to be the most fundamental. Following what is explicit in Bergson and Whitehead and at least implicit in Aquinas,[4] I take it that the first criterion should be the apparent agreement of the principles with what seems most fundamentally to be given within immediate experience. This is an appeal to philosophic intuition. The second criterion is the intrinsic coherence of the principles among themselves. Are they mutually consistent? And the third and final criterion consists in the success of the principles, taken together, in rendering experience intelligible, especially in ways not originally foreseen in the selection of the principles. Thus experience both grounds and, in the end, tests the selection of the principles invoked toward its understanding. But here there is no question of demonstration, since the issue lies in the choice of the very principles on which any philosophic demonstration could be based. It must instead lie in intellectual satisfaction with how the perspective as a whole illuminates experience.

3.4 THE PERSPECTIVE TAKEN HERE

Here I attempt to lay out the central principles that will dominate the following metaphysical interpretation of immediate experience as it has been roughly described above. As initial principles they cannot be demonstrated, but one has to start somewhere. I propose them as plausible but do not here undertake to argue for them other than to point to their apparent agreement with experience. Ultimately their plausibility must lie in their eventual success or failure to illuminate that experience.

Principle i

I accept, with Thomas Aquinas, that the *act of existing* (in Latin, *esse*) is the ground of all intelligibility and value, and hence is the basic ground from which any metaphysical explanation must proceed. Human experiencing is itself a particular instance of the act of existing. This notion of the act of existing, once intuitively grasped, powerfully illuminates everything else, yet is itself difficult to grasp because existing is not a thing or a quality or a form, and hence cannot be captured by a concept. Though it is the root of all intelligibility, the act of existing is itself conceptually invisible. Concepts are like intellectual snapshots. They designate timeless forms or characters and so cannot adequately capture activity in its flowing. Yet that is of the essence here: to grasp the act of existing which is a dynamic fulfillment, a *real-izing* of what would otherwise be only a potentiality for existing.

Principle ii

What is more, existing always entails *making a difference to others*. By its very nature, existing cannot be wrapped in isolation. It always entails the activity of affecting others. W. Norris Clarke has captured this notion within the single word *presencing*: it bespeaks both the dynamism of self-fulfillment and making a difference to others.[5]

Principle iii

In line with the above, I accept the Thomistic (and, in general, scholastic) distinction among three modes or aspects of existing: the act itself of *existing* (*esse*), the act of *coming into being* (*fieri*) of a substance or primary being,[6] and the consequent activity (*agere*) that flows from the act of existing. In this sense, being, becoming, and acting are conceptually distinguishable, though not concretely separable, aspects of existing. An existent, precisely as such, overflows its own self by acting on others; activity flows from existing as a particular mode of existing. Coming into being, however, as a true beginning, is not an event in any ordinary sense of the word, and is not itself temporal.

Principle iv

This notion of the act of existing entails an inner polarity, within the things that we experience, of the actual as the fulfillment of the possible. *All potentiality for further existing must reside in what is already actual.* Similarly, every actuality, of whatever sort, is grounded in some actual being. Such an affirmation, implicit in Aquinas and explicit in Leibniz and Whitehead, is usually called the *ontological principle,* and I accept it here. Thus, "possibles" do not exist on their own, and every finite actuality has the relation of fulfillment with respect to a previous potentiality latent within an actuality.[7] I thus accept the validity of the Aristotelian distinction between actuality and potentiality.

Principle v

Regarding *efficient causality,* I agree with Aristotle that the activity of the efficient cause lies precisely within its effect and not outside it. In that sense the cause is intrinsically linked to its effect, contrary to the philosophic conceptions prevalent since Hume.[8] I couple this intellectual analysis with Whitehead's original recognition that an intrinsic aspect of sense experiencing consists precisely in the *feeling* of the causal impact of other things of the world upon us, as well as the feeling of both the value dimension and the ongoing flow of experience from past through present to future.[9]

3.5 EXPERIENCING, NATURAL ACTIVITIES, AND AIMS

I now return to the assumption made in section 1.2, that human experiencing mirrors the fundamental structure of all natural activities. We saw that there are good general reasons for accepting it, but if we do, we take a step with singular and seemingly implausible consequences.

Principle vi

Regarding *aims* or *final causality,* and in accord with the principle enunciated in section 1.2, I assume that *all basic activities within nature are goal-directed,* aiming at some further fulfillment, although usually not consciously so. That is, since with Whitehead I accept that human experience is derivative from, and revelatory of, cosmic process in general, I also accept that all fundamental natural process is goal-aimed. I thus acknowledge that the ancient Greeks were right in their conception of nature as dynamic and teleological rather than mechanistic.[10]

Principle vii

The previous principle implies that a thoroughgoing teleological metaphysics has no place for a dead nature but rather presupposes that ideals for future value realization are in some way *experientially felt*. I am not speaking here of an experience that need be *conscious*. Most such experience is not. But to say that an aim causes precisely by "attracting" is to accept, with Whitehead and others, that the ultimates in nature are in some sense experiential, unlike the atoms of Democritus. And once again, if human experience is an outgrowth of the evolutionary process of the universe—if it is, in fact, that evolutionary process having come to the self-awareness of consciousness—then it is no surprise that through that very consciousness we recognize a basic experiential dynamism of cosmic process.

To the modern, scientifically trained ear principles vi and vii seem at first outrageous. Science has no place for aims or goals because it has no place for values. That is no criticism of science, just an acknowledgment of the necessary limitation of its horizon, a limitation that philosophy endeavors in its own way to overcome. Furthermore, evolutionary and biological theory may seem to have replaced teleological models with purely mechanistic and behavioral ones. So applying the teleological aspect of human experience to all activities in nature requires that we make plausible, at least, how such a view might even today be still coherently thinkable. This I propose gradually to do in later chapters, especially 10 through 13.

What in general would such an argument amount to? First, it should be noticed that the contemporary concept of "cause" is practically identified with "efficient cause," understood as deterministic. This has profound consequences for the controversy whether any human decisions can be free. Also, the usual transliteration of the traditional expression *causa efficiens* as "efficient cause" itself provokes another misunderstanding, since the modern word "efficient" tends to evoke the notion of practicality rather than of a specific type of influence. For that reason I prefer to render *causa efficiens* as "effective cause."

Now an interpretation of nature in terms of *final* causality is one ontological option among others, and I do not see how such a teleological solution could be either established or refuted taken just in itself. It rather forms an essential fabric of a whole metaphysical perspective, and it and the perspective stand or fall not only by the test of logical coherence but much more by the evident success of the entire perspective in illuminating the experience out of which it grew and which it is meant to render intelligible.

But what is the ontological character of any final cause or aim, especially as distinguished from an effective cause? The word "final" derives, of course, from the Latin word *finis,* which denotes not only completion but also, as in English, end in the sense of goal or aim. Now a final cause or aim causes precisely by attraction rather than by anything like an internal necessitation. (The latter would more properly be the function of an effective cause.)

The notion of causal attraction entails considerable ontological consequences. First, it requires that the aim has the character of value or importance with respect to that being that feels it as an aim. It is felt as a good that is achievable though not yet achieved. Second, I accept with Aquinas that the ultimate Source of good is *an unlimited act of existing,* what I shall in chapter 12 (section 12.1) call "Alpha." Consequently every finite aim defines a limited, hence determinate, orientation toward the act of existing. Putting it another way, aim defines a particular possible way of realizing existence, which realization would constitute an enrichment of the primary being that feels the aim.[11] Thus aim is the felt attractiveness of a particular, fuller participation in the act of existing, a possibility felt as available for realization by the primary being feeling the aim. In the next chapter I shall begin to address the question of how the "feeling" of an unrealized possibility is conceivable within the primary beings of the world.

Principle viii

Once again, in agreement with the principle of extrapolation from human experience and with the potentiality-actuality polarity within the act of existing (of which experiencing is an instance), I accept that *experiencing is an activity in existing of an experiencer, of a subject or agent doing the experiencing.* The act of experiencing is bipolar, constituting an intrinsic relation between the experiencer and that which is experienced. As I mentioned in the second chapter, experience gives itself as of a subject involved in a world. One's activity of experiencing is not free-standing but the activity of oneself as source and subject of the activity. Further, my activity of experiencing stands related to me the experiencer as actuality or fulfillment of me as a potential experiencer.[12] Consequently I cannot leave the experiencing subject out of even a rough metaphysical description of immediate experiencing such as I am about to attempt.

Chapter 4

A Preliminary Metaphysical Interpretation of Experience

4.1 THE BIPOLARITY OF EXPERIENCING

Experiencing is an activity in existing that reveals itself as bipolar: as of a subject engaged with objects in a world. *That* this is so is a matter of immediate feeling (Whitehead's perception in the mode of causal efficacy). But this sensible feeling of the causal impact of objects upon us is rendered intelligible in terms of the real existence of those objects as acting upon us through their effective causality. In accord with Aristotle's insight (enunciated in section 3.4 as principle v), the causal influence of those sensible objects lies precisely within our bodily senses and thus grounds the legitimacy of epistemological realism.

Here we have an example of the dynamism of existing, of *presencing*. I accept the authenticity of realism because only really existent entities (primary beings) are capable of acting upon us. That is, causal activity belongs solely to agents, existing sources of that activity (section 3.5, principle vii). Conversely, it belongs to primary beings to make a difference to others by means of their activity. And this is the metaphysical ground for our experience of being part of a world, of an ensemble of interacting primary beings.

4.2 THE EXPERIENCE OF VALUE

Experiencing is sensitive to value or importance, good or bad. This is immediately given and is a prerequisite for the goal-directedness that we actually experience in our deliberate actions. Framing this phenomenon in metaphysical terms, we recognize within the given situation a potentiality for realizing a desirable but presently nonexistent actuality. If, as I have presumed with Aquinas, existing is the ground of all value, then goal-directed activity aims at fulfilling or actualizing a more intense state of existing that now exists only as a potentiality.

This entails that in addition to recognizing the factuality of the world as it impresses itself upon us, we also feel relevant potentialities for existing in ways not yet achieved. It will remain to inquire more exactly into the existential status of such potentialities and how they can be experienced potentialities.

That such potentialities can become for us goals for activity requires in the first place that they be experienced as value-ordered. As goals, potentialities for existing are exactly potentialities for the realization of value. The whole concept of an aim or goal is that it be felt as a desirable but not yet realized actuality. This again fits the Thomistic concept that the ultimate root of value lies in the very act of existing.

Value relations, however, are essentially relative to some norm of greater or lesser value. Hence making sense of goal-directed activity requires on the part of the acting subject an intrinsic sensitivity to a norm of value against which the potentialities for the future are felt. In the next chapter we shall begin an examination of how this is possible.

In the second chapter we noted the experience of feeling the derivation of the present from the past and of the future from the present. One is free, of course, to interpret this as a purely subjective feeling. I propose however, with Whitehead, to accept the objective authenticity of this feeling of derivation. In that case one can interpret it as a sign of both the temporal structure of experiencing and of the causal connectedness of existents. Referred to the world, it indicates just that interconnectedness of activity that is entailed by existing. Referred to the experiencing subject, it manifests the temporal fabric of human existing. I retain my self-identity while at the same time find myself constantly developing over time within myself. The feeling of derivation provides a profound insight into the ongoing, temporal character of human existing.[1]

For it can be persuasively argued, I think, that the nature of immediate human experience entails the self-identity over time of a single experiencer. Experience as we find it would simply make no sense unless we suppose this kind of temporal self-identity of the experiencing subject.[2]

Such a conception of the experiencing subject is at odds with Locke's notion of "substance" as of a static, unchanging substrate underlying extrinsic qualitative changes. In that unfortunate conceptuality the substance or substrate does not itself change when acquiring or losing particular qualities any more than a person changes intrinsically by putting on or taking off clothing.

4.4 THE SUBJECT OF EXPERIENCING

These preliminary considerations underscore the necessity of giving an adequate account of the subject of experiencing if we are to give an account of experiencing itself. How are we to understand the ever-changing yet self-identical subject of ongoing experience? In the context of these considerations that is no ordinary question. For I have already proposed—with Bergson and Whitehead—to take human experiencing as paradigmatic, at least in its essentials, of the activity of all natural existents. Thus, to describe human experiencing, and especially to describe the ontological status of the experiencing subject, is in effect to describe the basic structure of every existent in nature. It is to raise once again the perennial philosophic question identified by Aristotle, who wrote: "The question that has always been asked and is still being asked today, the ever-puzzling question, 'What is being?' amounts to this: 'What is primary being?'"[3]

Here the translator has wisely rendered Aristotle's word *ousía*, which derives from the Greek word *to be*, as "primary being."[4] Primary beings, in this sense, are the true ontological units of reality, the ultimate things that are. How then can we describe the metaphysical structure of a primary being, using the model of the subject of experiencing?

Chapter 5

Aims and the Experiencing Subject

5.1 PROBLEMS

I assume that as a human being I am a primary being in the sense described in the previous chapter. I am a focus of existing and a source of acting. I am also aware that although I remain the selfsame me over time, I nevertheless constantly change internally without losing that self-identity. In addition, I recognize that I share the same fundamental nature with all other human beings, yet am an individual distinct from any of them.

Here we have no less than three interrelated problems for philosophic solution: (1) How can I share a common human nature with many others? (2) What fundamentally individuates me from all the other human beings? (3) In what ways can I differ from them in *what* I am without losing my basic character as human? The sense of these questions will become clearer as we struggle with them.

I find myself, within my experiencing, to be the selfsame me over at least some span of time. There is a unity in my existing and my acting—in my "presencing." This unity is twofold. There is the felt continuity of my act of existing flowing from the past into the present and issuing into a future. There is also a unity of what I call the *essential character* of that act of existing. This character as it were *filters* the act of existing to be just this or that sort. For the act of existing is not homogeneous among all kinds of existents, still less is it mere class inclusion. It is an activity that actualizes a particular kind of capacity by the richness of existing. The manner of existing of a human being, for instance, differs intrinsically from that of a horse. It does not stretch speech too far to say that humans exist more *intensely* than does a rock or a rose or a horse. Every act of existing, after all, is just the actual-izing of a particular, definite, and hence limited, capacity for existing in a certain way—what I have called the essential character of the primary being. The self-identity through time of a primary being entails that it retains its selfsame essential character. Thus it is necessary to distinguish this essential character from subordinate characters that have traditionally been called "accidental," such as race or sex.

How does it come about, however, that every primary being has an essential character, an effective unifying factor that constitutes it a primary being able to receive existence and consequently to function in a specific way? *I postulate* that my ultimate, determinate, unifying, and dynamic principle of being is precisely my *essential aim,* and that my *essential character* is ontologically derivative from that essential aim. Only because I find myself *dynamically aimed at existing in a human way,* with a kind of unlimited capacity for further intensifying, by my own activities, that manner of existing, do I find myself instantiating a specifically human essential character.

To repeat: I do not say that my aim derives from my human character; rather, my character as human derives from my aim.

In traditional terms, my formal cause, which constitutes me human, is a function of, and ontologically derivative from, my final cause, my essential aim.

Now, I did not always exist, but when I came into existence as the human person that is me (whenever exactly that took place from a biological perspective) I was in possession of the essential aim that defines me as human and that orients me toward my own fulfillment. What can be responsible for my possessing that defining aim?

Several possible answers to that question will be seriously considered in later chapters. Meanwhile it is enough here to rule out one answer as not possible at all: that I am myself the source of my own essential aim. For if, as I maintain, all my activities—for instance, the activity of evoking or inventing for myself an essential aim—are necessarily activities of me as a primary being and agent, then I cannot without circularity suppose that I myself, already constituted as an agent, produced by my own activity a principle that is a necessary condition for my being or acting at all. Rather, I must somehow be provided from without by that essential aim whereby I exist and act as a human being.

This givenness of the essential aim might at first sound like a fundamental obstacle to freedom. If I cannot freely choose my ultimate aim, how can I be free at all? But the objection rests on a misunderstanding. Every free act has to be goal-directed, for the aim or final cause is just the kind of cause that enables a choice without necessitating it. Lack of an essential aim would result in no activity at all. Thus the presence of the essential aim, far from inhibiting freedom, is just what makes the free act possible. Freedom resides in the particular acts that I originate *in virtue of* the essential aim.

5.3 INDIVIDUATION

I find myself one human being among billions of others, all equally human yet existing distinctly from me. How can I make philosophic sense of this distinction in unity? From a contemporary social perspective it is evident that giving a rational answer to this question is of far-reaching importance.

In terms we have thus far developed, the question becomes, How is it that I can have specifically the same essential character as do many others? It is instructive here to notice that it would be misleading to pose the question as, What makes me me? For that form of the question tempts one to muddle three very different questions: (1) what makes me a human being (rather than, say, a rabbit)?; (2) what makes me the *sort* of human person that I am? and (3) what principle is responsible for my having a numerically distinct act of existing from that of all other humans? The first question can be phrased as, What is the determinant of my nature? We have already suggested an answer to this in terms of essential character governed by essential aim. The second asks, What is the source of my particular individuality even as a human? The third asks, What individuates me, not qualitatively but numerically, from other humans?

This distinction of individuation from individuality is important. The dictionary defines individuality as "the sum of the characteristics that set one person or thing apart [from others]." That is, individuality is the sum of the *formal* ways in which one person differs from other given persons. But this already presupposes several individuated persons whose characteristics can be compared. The interesting question, however, is precisely how there can exist several individuated persons all of whom share the same essential characteristic, not different ones. They do not differ at all in their essential characters, yet their acts of existing are distinct from one another: the act of existing of primary being A is really distinct from the act of existing of primary being B.

The individuation of distinct primary beings that all share specifically the same essential character cannot be grounded in any *formal,* that is *qualitative,* characteristics. For if the qualitative characteristics amount to what I have called essential characters, then we do not have different beings of the same sort but different sorts of beings altogether. If however the qualitative characters are less fundamental than essential characters, they would be insufficient to account for a radical distinction of acts of existing. Such individuation must be due to some principle that is nonqualitative, a principle that in some sense is extraneous to anything like a character. This is difficult to grasp just because we so easily see the qualitative differences between black people and white, between males and females, that we overlook that our problem concerns how there can exist several distinct human beings in the first place, all of whom are equally human though they also happen to be black or white, male or female.

The only available answer to the question turns out to be also the obvious one: we inhabit different *bodies,* bodies that are, in the nature of things, set apart from one another by relations of *quantity.* The brute factuality of located, quantified bodies individuates them without touching their essential characters. True, the essential character of every human being requires some body or other, but it is essentially indifferent to having this particular, here-and-now body rather than some other. The particularity of bodily, space-time location is the ground of our numerical distinction as human beings and of our consequent differences in individuality.[1] How these quantitative relations may be conceived awaits consideration in a later chapter.

5.4 SUMMARY

Essential aim is the key principle constituting a primary being. It is not only the norm for all the being's immediate aims, it also governs the being's essential character inasmuch as that character is naturally ordered to that aim. Thus it ultimately determines what sort of being it is and how it acts.[2] For its activities are all aimed, each in its own way, at the essential aim, which is the aim at fulfillment of existing in its own particular way. I do not hesitate to propose with Whitehead, and indeed with Aquinas, that in fact *all natural activity is basically (though usually not consciously) goal-aimed.* If that be the case, then it remains to give an account of the presence in nature of essential aims. As I already remarked, in a thoroughgoing teleological metaphysics each primary being acts in virtue of an essential aim that it cannot itself have chosen but that must in some way be provided for it. How this can be thought possible remains to be considered.

Though the primary being cannot choose its own essential aim, it does choose for itself, throughout its life span, any number of more particular aims that are felt (sometimes mistakenly) as contributing to the achievement of its essential aim. What exactly constitutes that essential aim for us humans is not easy to specify, and we shall briefly consider it in the final chapter. In general it could be described, for all kinds of primary beings, as the aim at self-fulfillment, at maximal realizing of value. The particular, limited aims that the being constantly adopts for itself in virtue of its essential aim I call its *immediate aims.*

Aims, however, whether essential or immediate, cannot themselves account for the individuation of primary beings that have the same essential character, for what is needed in that case is a nonformal, in the sense of nonqualitative, principle of individuation. Such a principle is evidently found in the quantitatively distinct bodies identified with the primary beings. We shall attempt to begin, at least, an examination of bodies and quantity in the next chapter.

I have already referred to the old principle that if you want to know what a thing is, look at what it does. At this point we have not nearly completed an analysis of the structure of primary beings, and I propose that the best way to proceed farther is to look, in a later chapter, at what the interactions of primary beings reveal to us of their own structure.

Chapter 6

The Object-Structure of Immediate Experience: Space

6.1 IMMERSION IN A WORLD

I return once more to immediate experience and consider it more closely in its object-pole, in how it links us with an external, bodily world. I try at the same time not to lose sight of the hypothesis that the most fundamental structure of our own experiencing stands as a reasonable model for the basic structure of primary beings generally. For the sake of concreteness, but on the supposition that my experience is essentially like yours, I shall revert to using the first person singular.

Experientially I feel myself immersed in a world, a totality of other bodily beings that act upon my senses. This is a primitive experience and one of which, as we have seen, I can give a reasonable philosophic account. I experience myself as part of that world, that togetherness of bodies. This is, then, an experience of *unity within a plurality.* I experience many bodies, yet as forming a totality among themselves and a unity within my own experiencing of them. These bodies, and this world of bodies, I take to be real and extramental, though relational to me in my act of perceiving or understanding. The world that I encounter and analyze is an experienced world and its bodies are experienced bodies, not a world in itself nor bodies in themselves. My experience is of a multiplicity of bodies that yet form a unity within my experience. The experienced world is both many and one. How can I account for this?

I do not ask this question the way Kant did. I am not asking for the transcendental conditions of seeming to find a unified world in sheer phenomena. I rather am inquiring into the metaphysical requirements for the possibility of encountering within my experience an objectively structured unity in multiplicity.

6.2 THE CONTINUITY PROPER TO SPACE

I find the first element of an answer to this question in recognizing the existence, within my perceiving of objects, of a *principle of continuity* that is both *homogeneous and exclusive* (or more exactly, *exclusivizing*, if one permits the word). This principle provides a certain unity to the multiplicity of individual bodies and at the same time distinguishes them one from another. In the fifth chapter we encountered this same principle as essential to individuation. It is, of course, what we may for the moment call *space* or *quantity* or *extensiveness*.

It is a principle of continuity, but continuity of a particular kind. It is a continuity of *potential parts,* in that although it is a principle of continuity or wholeness, it lends itself to indefinite subdivision into actual parts. This is the continuity we all conceived in first encountering Euclidean geometry. It is a homogeneity in that its parts, potential or actual, do not differ from one another qualitatively but only in their standing apart from one another by the very fact of their being parts. Lengths of measurement (inches, seconds) are taken to be identical with one another and to differ only in their position within the continuity. That is the sense in which I referred to this continuity as *exclusive:* its parts exclude one another simply in being parts.

Kant was right in thinking that sense experience is unimaginable apart from space. He was wrong, I think, in supposing that the spatial structure of sense experience derives only from the mind rather than from the world—the experienced world. Here I must emphasize once again that I do not hold that in sense experience I encounter a world in itself. In fact I deny that. The world that I encounter is an extramental world as *perceived,* a world *as* related to me in the activity of perception, not a world in itself. I therefore take space to be an objective structure of that related world, for perceiving is an act that is not purely mental but consists in an interaction between me and the world. If that be the case, then we shall later have to examine more carefully the structure of the interactions among primary beings.

I thus agree with Leibniz[1] and Whitehead[2] in regarding space as not fundamental, as Descartes had thought, but rather as an objective condition of the interacting of primary beings. We form the abstract idea of space by recognizing the structure inherent in the ways in which we relate to the rest of the world and the world to us.

The space that I here speak of belongs to the horizon of ordinary sense perception. Its essential character is *a continuity of quantitative, exclusive homogeneity,* as I have explained. The mathematical realm of non-Euclidean geometries belongs to another horizon altogether, and I am not here concerned with it.

6.3 SPATIAL RELATIONSHIPS AS DERIVATIVE FROM EXPERIENCING

Spatial relationships, then, constitute that aspect of experiencing that makes one act of experiencing differ from another with the same essential character. These acts of experiencing, thus individuated, are the existential acts of distinct primary beings. And individuated primary beings as spatially related to one another are found in experience to be capable of moving with respect to one another.[3] This movement can be more or less intense, so to speak—faster or slower. Hence we come to the most common notion of *time,* defined by Aristotle as "the number [measure] of motion [of bodies] in respect of 'before' and 'after' [in the motion]."[4]

6.4 THE CONTINUITY OF OBJECT TIME

It is important to notice the characteristics of this most common conception of time. First, it explicitly measures the motion of *bodies* moving in space. It has nothing necessarily to do with other conceivable kinds of change, so that great caution should be exercised in attempting to apply it to them. Is it, for instance, a suitable concept for understanding human understanding? Only, presumably, if human understanding fits the paradigm of bodies moving in space. Second, time, so conceived, is found to share virtually all the characteristics of space as described above.[5] This kind of time, which I call object-time or clock time, is taken to be homogeneous (one minute like every other), quantitative (rather than qualitative), and exclusive (each part excludes every other just in virtue of being a part). But these are all the very characteristics that we attribute to space. Roughly the same can be said of the scientific notion of space-time—which is, in any case, not part of the natural perceptual horizon.

Object-time, however, is not the only viable concept of time. We turn now to a more fundamental concept that I call *subject-time.*

Chapter 7

The Subject-Structure of Immediate Experience: Time

7.1 SELF-IDENTITY OVER TIME

I maintained earlier (section 4.3) that the very notion of experiencing requires the self-identity over time of a single experiencer. No human experience is instantaneous, and I am aware, within my every act of experiencing, that I am the same experiencing-me throughout the experience. Though I think this is arguably true for any human experience whatever, it is perhaps more evident in the experience of the *derivation of the present from the immediate past.* Here I am aware of a developing-me even as I retain my self-identity. A stroboscopic succession of distinct "me's" simply does not seem to fit my experience.[1] Let us examine the experience of derivation more closely.

Once again it proves enlightening to do this in terms of the kind of *continuity* involved in the experiencing. What are the central characteristics of the continuity inherent in immediate experiencing? I suggest two of the most ordinary forms of experiencing as concrete examples for analysis. The first is the enjoyment of music, or even more simply, of hearing a melody. This is an activity that spans some measure of clock time. The dictionary defines a melody as "pleasing sounds in sequence," but that does not do it justice. This sequence of pleasing sounds or notes forms a unity or it would not be a melody. The notes of the sequence do not stand alone, as isolated one from another, but precisely as forming a unified whole. There is a togetherness of the notes or else there is no melody. Yet the notes can be played only one at a time. In the instrument or the concert hall—physically, in other words—the notes are isolated. All the former notes have already ceased to be produced by the time each succeeding note is played. Yet the human experience of a melody is of the notes as forming a unity, so that the previous notes have not in fact simply disappeared but are in some way *included in the ongoing present experiencing.* Indeed they even furnish a certain anticipation of the notes immediately to come.

But where are these past notes that yet exist despite their being physically gone? They are contained within the very act of experiencing, the act of hearing the melody. In one sense the past is simply gone. Yet, as St. Augustine speculated: "Perhaps it would be exact to say: there are three times, a present of things past, a present of things present, a present of things to come. In the soul there are these three aspects of time, and I do not see them anywhere else."[2] The present of the past resides "in the mind," in our very experiencing itself.[3]

I return, then, to the continuity involved in the experience of hearing a melody. There is indeed a continuity, for we experience the melody as forming a kind of whole. The difference between the individual notes is experienced as qualitative rather than quantitative. And finally, we find, paradoxically, that the present *includes* the past (and, in some way, also the future by anticipation) rather than excludes it. We have, then, in this simple act of experiencing *a continuity of inclusive, qualitative heterogeneity,* in exact contrast to the continuity of exclusive, quantitative homogeneity that we recognized in space and in object-time. The continuity of immediate experience is nothing like that of space or of the time measured by clocks.

The second concrete example exactly parallels the first: the ordinary experience of understanding spoken language. The words, or even the syllables, must be uttered individually, and in such a way that the previous words have physically ceased to exist by the time each following word is spoken. Yet if the previous words were not somehow still present, no meaning could be conveyed. Where, then, do the words of the sentence enjoy a unity if not in the very act of conscious experience? Once again this is a kind of continuous unity such that the present includes rather than excludes the past.

These two concrete examples exemplify the character of experiencing generally. Experiencing is an ongoing, qualitative flow that in a nonquantitative way includes the past within the present, together with a certain anticipation of the future.

Now does not this ongoing flow of experiencing exactly constitute *the time of our lives?* What extraneous measure could we impose upon it? Surely not object-time, and that for two reasons: first, experiencing is nothing like the motion of bodies in space; and second, its type of continuity is radically different from that of object-time. It seems, then, that ongoing experiencing is a kind of flow that measures our relation with the rest of the world rather than is measured by anything apart from itself. I therefore propose to call it *subject-time.* I shall argue later that it can rightly be regarded as the time of *agency* and the time of *freedom.*

It seems appropriate, as a final consideration concerning the subject-structure of immediate experience, to recall the evident *goal-directedness* of deliberate human activity. We directly experience aiming at a goal of value achievement, and we have argued that it is plausible to take the aim at a goal—though usually not entertained consciously—as typical of the activity of every primary being. Besides, we have argued that the very character of the primary being is a function of its essential aim, and also that all the immediate aims chosen by the primary being are dependent, by a kind of participation, on its essential aim. Everything therefore hinges around the notion of *aim,* and in particular of essential aim, though, as we have noted, essential aim cannot itself be the object of a primary being's choice. The being must rather have received its essential aim in some other way, possibly from the interaction of the other beings that make up its world.

What I now propose, in an unsophisticated way, is that aim also underlies our experience of *meaning*—or lack of it—in everything we do in our lives. The sense of (positive) meaning is just the feeling of moving toward, or of having achieved, our aims, especially our essential aim to the extent that it is achievable in any present.

All these considerations emphasize the need to give a more particular philosophical account of the interactivity of primary beings, and that is the topic to which we now turn.

Chapter 8

On the Interactions
of Primary Beings

8.1 WE AND THE WORLD

We experience ourselves as part of a world of sensible objects, of bodies of all sorts, that are not merely present to us but acting upon us as we also act on them. We live in a sea of causal interactivity. Let us attempt at least a preliminary metaphysical analysis of the interactions of primary beings in general, with a view to rendering more intelligible the structure of those beings and of the world they constitute.

Before beginning, however, it is necessary to forestall an obvious objection against the usefulness of such an undertaking. Since we are concerned with the interactions of bodies, it may seem foolish for philosophers to attempt any analysis different from what is being furnished so impressively by scientists. Would this not be a naive exercise in what is now abusively referred to as "folk psychology"?

This objection can best be met by enlarging on the notion of *perspectives,* which we briefly considered in the third chapter. Indeed I made a brief argument along this line when, in section 3.4, I defended principle vi, which asserts a universal goal-directedness in the activities of nature. Here, however, I wish to begin by recalling the epistemological basis on which the present analysis of interactivity will be carried out.

8.2 MORE ON RELATIONAL REALISM

Here I need to amplify the remarks on relational realism that I made in section 1.4. As a realism, this view holds that objects in a surrounding world constitute the normal, immediate objects of sense perception. This position opposes both an idealism, such as that of Berkeley, and a representationalism, such as that of Locke, Hume, and many others. We do not *infer* an external world from sense data, we *encounter* it *through* those data. There is a twofold ground for this claim. The first is the immediate feeling of being influenced in our sense organs by something outside us. Whitehead was right in taking this feeling of causal influence to be not only overlooked as part of the immediate experience of sensation but also to be authentic, as delivering what it purports to deliver. The problem then is to make philosophic sense of how this is possible.

The other ground lies in accepting the (Aristotelian) principle that the activity of the cause is found precisely in its effect. This of course contravenes Hume's gratuitous assertion that cause and effect must be altogether separate from each other. It is philosophically respectable to accept that the feeling of being *acted upon* in our sensing is exactly the feeling of the causal activity of external objects acting upon us.

The conclusion of this analysis is that in perception we find ourselves confronted neither with our own sense impressions as objects of perception, nor with external things as they are in themselves, but rather with external things *as they stand related to us in the act of perceiving*. We see neither appearances of an apple, nor an apple in itself, but an *appearing* apple through the mediation of the sense immutations it provokes in us.

8.3 PERSPECTIVES, HORIZONS, AND RELATIONAL REALISM

It is now clear that the diverse possible perspectives one can bring to perceiving or to knowing establish different horizons of intelligibility for the corresponding acts of perception or of knowing. The three persons looking at the same physical valley all *saw different valleys* because the valley each saw was a relational valley, not the valley-in-itself, and the relationship of the seen valley to each person was determined by the perspective of the person's interests. Thus the claim I made that diverse perspectives determine diverse horizons or fields of possible objects of knowledge exactly complements the contention that the objects of perception or of knowledge are necessarily relational objects, not objects in themselves.

For our present consideration there are just two perspectives of interest. The first is the perspective of *ordinary sensibility* by which we perceive the world around us, coupled with the accompanying perspective of *ordinary knowledge* by which we try to make immediate, intelligible sense of what we sensibly perceive. The second is the *scientific* perspective by which we draw inferences about an extramental world as it reveals itself to us, not indeed directly but only through our theoretic understanding of its interaction with our instruments.

In the introduction to his *Nature of the Physical World,* the English physicist Sir Arthur Eddington contrasted the ordinary table on which he was writing, a table that was smooth and hard and brown, with the scientific description of the same table. The scientific table was mostly emptiness in which electric charges rushed about with great speed. There were, he surmised, not one but two tables: the everyday, perceptible table and the scientific table. He then went on to write: "I need not tell you that modern physics has by delicate test and remorseless logic assured me that my second scientific table is the only one which is really there."[1]

But Eddington's paradoxical conclusion of the unreality of the sensible table arose from muddling the ordinary and the scientific perspectives along with their horizons of possible objects of knowledge. Through our senses we do indeed encounter the (relational) table as smooth and hard and brown, and this is all that we could want or expect in a sensed table. But the "scientific table," determined by the scientific, instrumental perspective, belongs to quite a different epistemological horizon from the common-sense table on which we write.

Applying these ideas to our present problem, we see that we are justified in giving a metaphysical analysis of the interactions of primary beings as we observe them in ordinary sense experience without being embarrassed that we are not physicists or biologists. In fact it would be a major philosophic error to reduce all knowing to that of the horizon attainable by science. What the physicist says and what the philosopher says are not contradictory but complementary to each other.

8.4 ESSENTIAL AIM AND OUR RELATION TO THE WORLD

In chapter six we identified space as the nonqualitative, homogenous, exclusive principle of continuity in virtue of which bodies are individuated from one another, share a common world, and are capable of being in motion with respect to one another. It is thus that all of us recognize ourselves as related to a surrounding world. Again, we have noted that our immediate experience of that world includes the feeling of being acted upon by it, and is also a spur to react to it in a way of our own choosing. The possibility of such reaction is grounded in our feeling of the relative value of the various possibilities for reaction with respect to our essential aim. Only in virtue of that essential aim do we constitute one of those possibilities an immediate aim for action.

From moment to moment, then, we find ourselves called upon to react to the world around us in a way meant to contribute to our essential aim. In response to the causal activity exerted upon us by our surrounding world we ourselves react causally to it. In accord with our common-sense feeling of freedom in our activity, I submit that our reactions to the world, though indeed strongly influenced in many ways, are not in fact determined or necessitated either in our reacting at all or in our reacting in some determinate way.[2] Rather, in reacting we literally *originate* the activity, we create an activity for which the ultimate *reason* lies precisely in *us as acting*.

It will be obvious how the possibility for such origination is grounded in the essential aim of the acting primary being. Only in virtue of the attraction of that aim can the activity arise. The general character of the activity is that of *constituting* some particular, recognized possibility for action to be an *immediate aim* for action in view of its relation to the essential aim that underlies every activity of the primary being.

8.5 THE TEMPORALITY OF OUR ACTIONS

We initiate our reaction to the world by some movement of our bodies. In so doing we are causally affecting the surrounding bodies. What is to be said about the temporal aspect of the action of the world upon us and of us upon the world?

It has long been assumed, notably by Whitehead and probably by the majority of recent philosophers as well, that Einstein's epistemological conception of simultaneity is to be accorded even ontological validity, so that contemporary events, by definition, cannot affect one another. The consequence of this assumption is that the only entities, the only world, that we can perceive is a past world, never the contemporary world. Elementary astronomy furnishes abundant examples:

when we see a street lamp, the moon, the sun, a planet, a star, and a galaxy we are seeing them not as they are now but as they were, respectively, a tiny fraction of a second ago, a few seconds ago, and so forth even to billions of years ago. This calculation, of course, is based on our knowledge of the finite speed of light and on an accompanying assumption, in accord with the Special Theory of Relativity, that no action, hence no signal from one body to another, can exceed the speed of light.[3]

Since we are here concerned with how one primary being can affect another, let us examine more carefully the common assumption that the cause can never be simultaneous with its effect. Consider the following observations.

(a) The ordinary, contemporary conception of causality is already deeply colored by Hume's contention, on what he takes to be obvious logical grounds, that cause and effect are events that are entirely distinct from each other, so that nothing of the one could possibly reveal anything of the other. Furthermore Hume rendered discovery of any such connection an epistemological impossibility by his arbitrarily narrow definition of what could be contained in a sense impression.

(b) Aristotle's observation that the causal activity of the cause lies in its effect should be taken seriously here. If that is the case, then the cause, *precisely in its causing,* has to be *simultaneous* with its effect.

(c) I couple this with the position of relational realism defended above. What I—or any primary being—encounter in perception by means of the acting of the object upon my sense organs, is never the object in itself but the object as related to me in the causal activity of perception. In direct perception, then, I perceive objects as *present* to me in their activity, not as past, because the objects I perceive are not objects in themselves but relational objects, objects as encountered in the activity of perception. These objects are *encountered as present,* as simultaneous with me in their causal activity. Only by an indirect process of inference do I conclude that I am seeing the galaxy as it was a million years ago. But I do not *perceive* any galaxy except as it relates to me *now* in my perception.

It will be recalled that in the epistemology of relational realism, although the only objects that I experience are relational objects, objects as related to me in the act of perception, nevertheless I am justified in judging that the objects that have thus acted upon my sense organs enjoy an autonomous existence of their own. Otherwise they could not have acted upon me. I can, of course, never in my perceiving catch an object being just itself, but I am justified in attributing an in-itself-ness to the perceived object (though not *as* perceived).

This same reasoning can be applied to the simultaneity of causing with its effect. Although the experienced-galaxy is encountered as present to me, I am justified in attributing to it both an autonomous existence and, for good scientific reasons, a pastness in that existence.[4]

8.6 RELATIONAL REALISM AND RELATIVITY

Speculation about thus visiting the past when observing distant galaxies is not uncommonly attended—at least among us nonscientists—with the tacit assumption of a single space-time manifold in which all events take place and in every moment of which there is a unique configuration of the universe. We may thus suppose that we can conceptually, at least, visit the past much as we visit fossils in a museum of natural history. We think of a definite past sequence of cosmic "nows," exact states of the universe. But relational realism agrees with relativity theory in denying the existence of any nonperspectival (nonrelativistic) state of the universe. Every "state of the universe" implies a description of it, and every description is necessarily perspectival, relative to the viewpoint from which it is experienced or described, and every act of experiencing and every description is perspectival, including the perspective constituted by its situation in space and in object-time.

If concreteness lies in actuality, then it is clear that the *unity* of the universe lies precisely in the interactivity of primary beings. It is a dynamic unity, not an abstraction. The feeling of such interactivity gives rise to what Whitehead called the feeling of World or of Totality or of the Whole.[5] This also agrees with Aquinas's contention that it flows from the very nature of an existing being that it *act*.[6]

8.8 THE CONCRETENESS OF INTERPERSONAL RELATIONSHIPS

I conclude this chapter with a proposal that may at first appear controversial. I propose that our most fundamental human experience is *interpersonal*. Relating to other persons is as concrete as we can get. This contention of course contradicts epistemological representationalism and materialistic reductionism, according to which we attain other persons only inferentially and indirectly. Contrast this with Whitehead's more astute observation (quoted above, section 2.7) that we don't go behind this relationship, we begin with it.

I accept Whitehead's view and ask what the immediate fact of interrelating with other persons reveals to us about ourselves and our world. The topic is too large to pursue here in any detail, but at least three factors seem to stand out immediately. They are the centrality of *value,* of *aim,* and of *human freedom.* Human relationships are founded, above all, on perceived value, which is the basis of respect, of friendship, and of love. Value is also what makes an aim to be an aim, something worth striving for, and it is characteristic of activity, especially of deliberate human activity, that it seeks an aim. That notion of deliberateness, however, implies that a truly human activity has its primal origin in the acting person, not in circumstances, and that in those very circumstances the person might have chosen differently. We know too little about love,

AIMS |

but we do know this: the acts of love cannot be coerced; if they are not given freely they do not deserve the name.

Paramount, then, in any consideration of human inter-relationships is the long-debated question about the meaning and existence of human freedom. This is, in fact, a classic meta-physical problem on which there is an enormous literature and little agreement. In the following chapter I sketch what seems to me to be a reasonable way of thinking about human freedom.

Chapter 9

Free Acts

9.1 HUMAN AGENCY

Specifically human acts—as distinguished from acts that merely happen to be done by a human being, such as sneezing—are deliberate, which is to say aware and free. They have their primal origin in *the person as acting.* The free act is ontologically subsequent to and transcendent of all the previous factors entering into the deciding, such as motives, proclivities, and conditioning. When all the latter have been taken into account, there remains the act of deciding— deciding for this conceived possibility rather than that, or even for acting at all—and this act is one of *origination,* of producing a new fact in the universe for which not the motives and tendencies but the acting person alone is responsible. That is the essence of the notion of *agency* that will pervade all the following discussion.

The following considerations, then, are directed toward better understanding free agency, so conceived. The freedom I have in mind is neither social nor political but individual. Also I am not interested in discussing *external* freedom, by which I mean the ability to carry out what we have chosen to do.[1]

External freedom is doubtless important to us all, for that is what we lose by jail cells or handcuffs. But I am here concerned to examine the plausibility of the existence of an *internal* freedom, a freedom by which we internally make a *choice or decision* about some sort of action, regardless of whether it is possible for us to carry it out. We take a stand; we opt for a conceived aim.

9.2 BELIEF IN UNFREEDOM

It seems both curious and regrettable that the majority of contemporary philosophers in one way or another deny the existence of this internal freedom. Yet it is hard to believe that they always held that opinion. Children instinctively, even obstinately, maintain their own ability to choose, even when under heavy parental pressure. How then do they in later years come to disbelieve in that freedom? Because, I surmise, they encountered various traditional arguments that purport to show that internal freedom is an impossibility and an illusion. It is fair, then, to ask what is the most reasonable stance to take regarding any arguments for or against freedom. What might be proved or disproved, and what in the end seems the most reasonable criterion for affirming or denying freedom?

9.3 FREEDOM AND UNFREEDOM NOT DEMONSTRABLE

With regard to this latter question I submit that it is not possible demonstratively to prove either that we are free in the above sense or that we are not free. To insist, for instance, that every choice we make *must* have been determined by the preponderance of all our motives and previous conditioning is not to state an evident fact but simply to make a linguistic power play that closes a case by decree. But neither is it possible to prove demonstratively that we *are* free. Our only option is to accept the view that on the whole seems to be the more reasonable interpretation of our experience. In the following few paragraphs I shall argue that it is reasonable to suppose that, at least sometimes, we do actually exercise this internal freedom that we seem to feel.[2] I am not here concerned to show that it is plausible we are free in every single act. But if I can show, as I propose to do, that it is reasonable to think that we are free in at least some acts, I shall have discredited most of the arguments for determinism.

9.4 THE BASIC CAUSAL ARGUMENT AGAINST FREE ACTS

In this short space it is neither possible nor necessary to review all the particular arguments that can be raised against the authenticity of internal freedom, freedom in the very act of deciding or choosing. To every argument there is a reply that is at least plausible.[3] If, for instance, one were to argue that every decision must simply be the vector sum of all the motives preceding it, on analogy with the composition of forces in elementary physics, one can perfectly reasonably deny the parity. But there is one argument that seems to me to lie behind almost all the others, and it is an argument that takes us to the core of the metaphysical issue.

This argument is based on causality, and runs something like this. Every deliberate choice, in the sense of decision, is either caused by the antecedent motives, taken together with the proclivities of the chooser, or it is not. If the former, then the choice is necessitated by those motives and so cannot be considered free in the sense usually required for responsibility and moral worth. If it is not thus determinately caused, then the choice is a-causal (or as is sometimes said, contra-causal): it simply *happens*, literally for no reason at all, and so once again it is not free in terms of the freedom requisite for responsibility and morality. In neither case, then, can any act of choice have the freedom necessary for responsibility.

Given that dilemma, a great many philosophers have revised their view of what is necessary for responsibility. They have accepted that the only freedom worth having is in fact compatible with the determinate necessity of the outcome. Freedom (in their sense) is compatible with determinism, and so they call their position *compatibilism.* To cite Locke's own example: I might find myself in a locked room and so not free to leave it, while at the same time I wholeheartedly desire to stay in that room so as to be with another person who is also in it.[4] Thus freedom and determinism can coexist, and compatibilism seems to win the day.

But this easy solution works only just so far as we arbitrarily restrict the notion of freedom to what I call *external* freedom, the ability to carry out what one chooses. That notion of freedom, however, is not philosophically interesting. Whether one could succeed in leaving the room if one chose to do so may be a question for a locksmith, but the philosophic problem is whether one can be free so to choose.

The above argument against internal freedom is, I have said, an argument based on causality: if the motives cause the decision, then the decision is not free; if they do not, then the decision simply happens, for no reason at all, and so is again not free in any reasonable sense. What is to be noticed, however, is that the concept of causality implicit in the argument is narrow and deterministic. The implicit assumption is that a cause necessitates its later effect, and that apart from such necessitation there is nothing but pure chance.

This arbitrarily narrow concept, however, overlooks the difference between effective and final causality and in so doing effectively dismisses the function of the latter. Yet the final cause or aim is the cause behind all the other types of cause; it is exactly the kind of cause that by its nature need not be deterministic. For *an aim causes by attraction,* not by impulsion. It can thus enable an activity without necessitating it.

The above argument against freedom also overlooks the possibility of a causation by *origination,* by *bringing about* something new and radically unforeseeable. It assumes that whatever is not necessitated must have blindly happened as a matter of pure chance. The argument also tacitly assumes that all the ingredients of producing the effect, all the factors of the cause, must temporally *preexist* the effect. It takes for granted that the act of deciding cannot be simultaneous with the decision reached.

9.5 THE CONCEPT OF FREE AGENCY

In the end the central point of controversy is this: *whether the very notion of free agency is rationally conceivable.* Is it thinkable that the ultimate factor in reaching a particular decision lies neither in the field of motives, nor in previous circumstances, nor in the dispositions of the agent, but in the agent's very act of deciding? The supposition latent within the notion of internal freedom is that, given *all* the motives, conditions, and dispositions, the agent may yet decide A rather than not-A, and settling on A is not due to the intrusion of still another motive. The reason for finally deciding on A lies precisely in the agent's activity of settling on it, and thus the responsibility for the decision lies with the *decider deciding,* not in any congeries of factors such as motives.

If what I have just asserted is reasonable, then we see that the free act, when it occurs, is an act of *origination,* a kind of creation. It brings into actuality something entirely new and hence radically unforeseeable inasmuch as the ultimate deciding factor does not precede but is simultaneous with the deciding act.[5]

I conclude, then, that this notion of *originative causal agency,* so very different from the usual contemporary notion of causality, makes rational sense of human freedom. In the light of this concept, and in view of our natural feeling of freedom, it is more reasonable to think that we are free, at least sometimes and under some circumstances, than to think that we never are. But accepting this conclusion requires abandoning the usual narrow conception of causality in favor of a wider and richer one, the notion of agency. It also requires acknowledging the central function of *aim* in enabling, while not necessitating, the agent to reach a decision for which the agent in its acting is alone responsible.

9.6 FREEDOM IN NATURE

The above considerations have dealt with specifically human freedom, mainly because we have immediate experience of it. But in accord with our procedure in this essay, I have reason to suppose that something analogous to human freedom obtains in nonhuman activities, to a greater or lesser extent. With Whitehead I assume some degree of freedom in all activity, and this assumption is obviously linked to the assumption of the universality of value dimension and goal-directedness (aims) in nature.

Chapter 10

The Basic Structure of Primary Beings

10.1 CONSIDERATION ON METHOD

At this point I revert to Aristotle's famous comment, already quoted in section 4.4: "The question that has always been asked and is still being asked today, the ever-puzzling question, 'What is being?' amounts to this: 'What is primary being?'" Though with Aquinas (and Heidegger) I agree that there is a yet more profound question to be posed, the question of the very act of existing itself, it is appropriate now to inquire into the structure of the basic units of existence, which I call primary beings, in view of the principles adopted above. Among these principles, the following are paramount:

(a) That immediate human experiencing reveals something of the ultimate structure of any primary being.

(b) That while existing, becoming, and acting (*esse, fieri,* and *agere*) are conceptually distinguishable though concretely inseparable aspects of being, to ask for the structure of a primary being is primarily to inquire into its capacity for *existing* (*esse*), without neglecting the other two aspects.

(c) That the *essential character* and even the life span of a primary being is determined by its *essential aim,* which essential aim cannot be provided by but rather given for the primary being (section 5.2).

(d) That through effective causality the surrounding world actively conditions the possibilities for response of the primary being, and that through both final and effective causality the primary being responds creatively (with a certain degree of freedom) to that world.

(e) Finally, that the concept "primary being," as that of the ultimate metaphysical unit of existing and acting, is abstract and hypothetical. I am not aware that we have any unquestionable, direct experience of a *simple* primary being. Probably the only primary being of which we are directly aware is our own self, but this self is undoubtedly complex. The question to be examined in later chapters is whether this complexity is a complexity simply of principles of being (as Aquinas supposed) or rather somehow a complexity of subordinate primary beings.

In light of the above principles, I postulate first of all that every primary being takes its *essential character* and is lured to its activities by its *essential aim* (in some ways similar to Whitehead's subjective—or initial—aim). Thus the essential aim governs the manner of existing of the primary being, including its thrust toward its own future. Essential aim, I propose, furnishes for the primary being its own ideal of self-fulfillment in existing and experiencing. This ideal is not so much an essence to be achieved as a vector toward fullness of *esse* in the being's determinate capacity for acting. For humans as such this would above all be intelligent and free activity toward other humans. Thus essential aim is both the perfective principle within the primary being and also its capacity for the act of existing and its resultant activities.

These relationships are illuminated by recalling that, as I have argued, no primary being can possibly provide for itself its own essential aim. Zebras don't choose to be zebras, nor we to be humans. We do choose, however, within human limits, what *sort* of human beings we shall be and, again within limits, how we shall act to fulfill our essential aim. Where essential aims come from is a difficult question that we shall address in some detail in a later chapter.

10.2 EXPERIENCING AS AN ACT IN EXISTING

The experiencing of the primary being is an *act in existing* (*esse*) with a subject-object polarity, in which the world is immediately present to the primary being in and through its activity upon that being. Whitehead appropriately refers to this experiencing as *feelings* on the part of the being: feelings of the factuality of the world as it lays its hand on the being in determinate ways. For Whitehead, in fact, the feelings are ontically antecedent to the being that emerges from the feelings. I on the contrary am presupposing the existence of the primary being that is doing the feeling. For the purpose of this analysis, *how* that very primary being comes to be is a related but distinct question that I shall deal with later. I therefore hypothetically presuppose, for this stage of analysis, a constituted primary being engaged in its feelings of the world.

10.3 EXPERIENCING POSSIBILITY

Ingredient in the being's feeling of the factualities of the world is also its feeling of the *form of definiteness* characterizing those actualities. It is a feeling of the ontological pattern exemplified in the fact. Concomitant with that is the feeling of the *derivation* of the present experience from the past and of the present as giving birth to a future. But beyond that there is also the feeling, to a greater or lesser degree, of the form of what, given the situation, *could be but is not yet*. It is the feeling of an unrealized, determinate *possibility* for the future, and in particular a feeling of a possibility of enhancement of value. It is precisely a feeling of *aim*.

I have argued for the plausibility of this universal teleology in section 3.4, principle vi. In section 5.4 I noted the need for distinguishing between the *essential aim* of the primary being and its *immediate aims*. The essential aim is not chosen by, but rather given for, the being, yet only in *virtue* of it—in the root sense of through its power—does the being choose its immediate aims as moving itself toward gradually fulfilling its overarching essential aim.

10.4 AIMS AND THE UNIVERSE

A requirement for the aims thus felt—both the essential aim and the immediate aims—is that they be consonant with the structure of the universe, otherwise there would simply be chaos. Yet chaos is not what we mainly observe. Harmony with the structure of the universe is necessary for essential aims if novel instances of value are successfully to emerge, as we see in the case of evolutionary advance. As to particular, immediate aims, we repeatedly experience how fallible and precarious the choices of the primary being can be.

10.5 THE REACTION OF THE PRIMARY BEING

Following upon its feeling of other primary beings and of their forms or patterns of existing, together with its feeling of the derivation of its present situation from its immediate past, the primary being responds more or less creatively—that is, with a greater or lesser degree of freedom. In chapter 9 I provided a basic defense of the reasonableness of maintaining some degree of freedom in human acts of deciding, and in section 3.4 I argued for principle vi, which asserts that all activity is to some degree goal oriented. But aiming at a goal presupposes that that goal, as a possibility for the immediate future, is in some way experienced, felt. It presupposes that the primary being feels not only the factual world, with its forms of definiteness, but also *attractive possibilities for what is not yet.*

We must distinguish two kinds of such possibilities. One is the overriding possibility for complete self-fulfillment, whatever that may be. That is what I have called the being's essential aim. It is, as it were, the felt ideal of the being's own self as come to its utter perfection. The other kind embraces the more particular possibilities for a response to the given situation, a response that is felt to be presently contributive to the essential aim. This is what I have called an immediate aim. The primary being more or less freely chooses its own immediate aims in virtue of its feeling of its own ultimate or essential aim which it did not choose.

10.6 "WHERE" ARE POSSIBILITIES FOR THE FUTURE?

The ontological principle defended in section 3.4, principle iv, demands that these as yet unrealized possibilities for the future—both essential and immediate aims—be grounded in one or more primary beings. They cannot float into experience from nowhere. Thus the "where" of these possibilities that are felt as immediate aims must lie in one or more primary beings.

To consider first the provenance of *immediate* aims, we ask whether the primary being that develops itself through these immediate aims can itself be the source of these particular aims. Does it invent its immediate aims, or rather recognize and adopt them? (Keep in mind that we are not here inquiring into the origin of *essential* aims, a topic that we shall have to address at some length in a later chapter.)

I postulate that the primary being is able, in virtue of the attraction of its essential aim, to contrive or invent particular patterns of possibilities, the pursuit of which would presumably contribute toward the achievement of its self-ideal or essential aim. This is equivalent to acknowledging that primary beings are capable, in varying degrees, of introducing novelty into the world. Whether such novelty is in fact consistent with the larger processes of the universe determines whether they survive in the evolutionary advance of nature.

10.7 THE SELF-MODIFICATION OF A PRIMARY BEING

In responding to its felt world through inventing and responding to its immediate aims, the primary being *modifies itself without ceasing to be itself,* without losing its own self-identity. This fits Aristotle's own concept of primary being (*ousía,* misleadingly translated as "substance"). Contrary to what has been mistakenly supposed by Whitehead and other process philosophers, Aristotle (also Aquinas) supposes that the *ousía itself* changes when it undergoes "accidental" (that is, nonsubstantive) transformations.[1] More exactly, in the present theory the primary being modifies its own feeling of its essential aim in choosing its immediate aims. In this way the primary being changes itself internally in time, yet without ceasing to be its same self. This process of self-development may rightly be called a kind of *becoming.* The other kind of becoming that we shall have to consider is the transition over time of successive primary beings.

10.8 SIMPLE AND COMPLEX PRIMARY BEINGS

By a "simple" primary being I mean one that is not made up of subordinate primary beings that, in a way about to be discussed, nevertheless constitute the primary being as a true unity rather than a sheer multiplicity. If the hypothetical primary being here under discussion is simple in the above sense, it seems reasonable to suppose that its aims, and consequently its response to its world, are relatively primitive and repetitive rather than productive of novelty. Thus the simple primary being may be suited merely to repeat itself in its successors. Whitehead suggests that this is what underlies the vibratory aspects of inorganic processes.[2]

Let us now consider how we may conceive more complex primary beings and thus approach more closely to the beings of our own experience. I am inclined to agree with Aristotle and Aquinas that animals can be taken as ontological unities precisely because they act as unities: their parts tend to cooperate both in health and in sickness toward the good of the individual and of the species. There can, of course, be no knockdown argument for this, but it seems the more plausible view if it can be shown intelligible. Above all I suppose that, in terms of the above metaphysics, I am myself a single (I did not say simple) primary being. I take as authentic my immediate awareness of self-identity in my life and activities, provided at least that I can plausibly make sense of it.

At the same time it is obvious that there is a complexity within my unity. My body alone has many interacting parts. Is there a way to make philosophic sense of a true ontological unity comprising this complexity? The water in my blood seems really to be water. How then can it be part of a unitary me?

This is of course an instance of the perennial philosophic puzzle of reconciling the One and the Many. It is a problem that is particularly acute for Whitehead's conception of reality in terms of metaphysical event-atoms, his actual entities or occasions of experience.[3] It may be thought that the problem was less acute for Aquinas (or for Aristotle) since Aquinas thought of the complexity not in terms of smaller units of being, each having its own character, but of *principles* of being that are not themselves little beings (any more than the principles of a watch are little watches). As for components that appear to retain the same individual identity within the human body as they have outside it, Aquinas could at best grant them a "virtual" existence of their own within the body, since every true component of the body had to take its character and activity from the body's single substantial form or soul.[4] To put it in modern terms, Aquinas would say that what appears to be water in the blood is not in fact water but only acts as if it were. (This is his theory of "virtual existence.")

Our present theory has an exact and, I think, better way of accounting for our own complexity. The essential aim governs the essential character, the individuality or self-identity, of every primary being. If then we are to find an ontological unity in a complexity of subordinate entities we must relate their own essential aims in such a way as *to subordinate all their aims to that of the unitary primary being.*[5] This subordination must be more than merely formal, a mere similarity of aims. Such a purely formal subordination could be just extrinsically functional, as in a clock or an automobile engine. We need, rather, to think of an *ontological dependence* of the aims of the subordinate entities on that of the primary being in such a way as to form an organic unity.

10.9 THE PARTICIPATION OF AIMS

In my *Coming To Be,* section 4.1j, I suggested that the aims of the subordinate entities in a complex primary being could be thought of as *participating in* the essential aim of the primary being. I wish now to reaffirm that suggestion and in a later chapter to discuss more fully how this may be possible. I shall also attempt to show how the ontological unity of a complex primary being consists in the participative harmony of the essential aims of all the subordinate entities with the essential aim of the primary being itself. In this way *the unity of the complex primary being is essentially teleological,* a kind of genetic sharing in the dominant essential aim and consequently in its essential character and its activity.

I thus conceive primary beings singly to exercise unitary existential acts of both experiencing and reacting to the world in virtue of an aim (not usually conscious) toward self-fulfillment. Their essential character is determined by that given aim, and in their response to the world they exercise some degree of free agency, especially in their adopting immediate aims as means contributory to their essential aim. Probably all the primary beings that we sensibly experience are complex inasmuch as they comprise numerous subordinate entities that, although relatively distinct in their particular activities, yet form an ontological unity by reason of their participation in the essential aim of the primary being as a whole.[6]

Chapter 11

Existing as Participated Act

11.1 TWO METAPHYSICAL PERSPECTIVES

At the very beginning of his *Introduction to Metaphysics* Martin Heidegger pointedly asks, "Why is there any existing thing at all, and not rather nothing?"[1] He is not asking why things are the way they are, but why are they at all. That, he claims, is the most fundamental of all questions, the Question of questions. And at the beginning of *Being and Time* he asserts that attention to the question of the very meaning of Be-ing is precisely what has been neglected in Western philosophy. After Parmenides and Heraclitus, that question became eclipsed by the more tractable question of the structure of particular sorts of beings.

I think that Heidegger was basically right, though he failed to notice that Aquinas had given a significant answer to the first question. In our above considerations we have devoted some attention to the presumed structure of what I have called primary beings. Let us now consider, in terms of our developing metaphysics, how it is that any primary beings exist at all.

In his above statements Heidegger implicitly defined two metaphysical horizons: one of the meaning of being itself, the other of the structure of beings. The latter naturally lends itself to accounting for the development through time of particular primary beings. I find it convenient to refer to this as the "horizontal" or temporal dimension of becoming. The former I call the "vertical" dimension, either of coming to be simply, which is not a temporal process at all, or of ongoing and continued dependence in existing. This is clearly the more fundamental dimension and it deserves some treatment at this stage of our thought.

11.2 PARTICIPATION IN EXISTING

I know of no more fundamental philosophic perspective than Aquinas's conception of *existing as a participated act*. Certainly this stands as the core of his philosophical view, though here is not the place to demonstrate that claim.[2] But I am convinced that Aquinas was right about this, and so I accept his view and wish to incorporate it here.

To grasp this perspective it is necessary to come to the understanding—intuition if you will—that *existing* is an *act*, even a kind of *activity*. Thus I am not talking about "existing" understood simply as a property of belonging to a logical class of objects (the class of those things that can be said to be extramentally real, in distinction from the class to which unicorns belong). If something is in fact real—such as a race horse—it is real *in virtue of, by reason of,* the activity to which I am trying to call attention. True, this is an "activity" unlike any other because it is the basic activity—the Ur-activity, if you will— by reason of which any other kind of activity is possible. Let me try to illustrate this from the thought of Aquinas, first by a trivial, contrived example, then by recourse to his theory of participation.

The contrived example is this. The verb "to be," whether in English or in Latin (or most any other language), is usually employed merely as a copula, a joiner that links the predicate to the subject of the proposition. Thus when we say "This grass is green" we commonly take the "is" simply to link the quality "green" as predicate to the grass as subject of the proposition. And Aquinas was not averse to writing this way. But I submit that it would better express his general metaphysical perspective to say, unusually, "This grass is greenly." That is a different and metaphysically more revealing assertion. For it is far less fundamental to suppose that a quality belongs to the substance grass, than it is to think that this grass is exercising its act of existing in a green sort of way. Aquinas habitually focuses his philosophic concentration precisely on that act of existing.

This is seen at its most powerful in his pervasive doctrine of *participation in the act of existing.* Here he borrows something from Plato and something from Plotinus, but creates his own original interpretation. Plato had conceived of participation in the Forms or ideal patterns of existence. For him the rose, the sunset, or the human body are beautiful just because, and only insofar as, they participate or share in the unique Form which is Beauty Itself. Plotinus had the insight that there are different levels of intensity of being (my expression, not his), and that the less intense beings are subordinate to, even somehow derivative (by a kind of emanation or flowing forth) from, what is most being or even beyond being itself, that is, The One. Emanation however was not thought of as a process taking place in time but rather as an atemporal, hence unchanging, relationship of subordination in levels of being.

Coupled with emanation, however, Plotinus also conceived a contrary and simultaneous vector of "return" by which each entity felt an inbuilt orientation back toward The One. For the human soul this return amounted to an ascetical vocation.

The notion of participation in existing is best seen, as I have said, in Aquinas's understanding of creation. That is why I adduce it here, though with some trepidation lest my referring to it be misunderstood. At the moment I am only trying to clarify the notion of participation in existing. I am not hereby accepting or trying to prove the existence of God as Aquinas doubtless conceived of God. Aquinas, after all, was writing primarily as a Catholic theologian as well as a philosopher, and so found it comfortable to identify the Source of participative existing as God. I shall later, and in a qualified sense, do the same, but it would be beyond my argument to do it now. So I ask leave of the reader simply to consider the content of the idea of creation, as Aquinas understood it, without at the moment making any claims with regard to God's actual existence.

Creation, as understood in the Scholastic tradition, is an "act" unlike any other, for it usually connotes a beginning that is in no sense an end of any previous state. It does not take place in time, but in constituting a material world of change it thereby constitutes the beginning of cosmic time. Creation effects a *coming to be,* pure and simple, that is not at all a becoming.[3] But although the notion of a beginning is usually implied in the word "creation," the essence of creation consists rather in *a relation of constant causal dependence on a Source Being for the very existing of the created being.* Thus although "creation" normally implies the beginning of this relation of existential dependence, the very same dependence necessarily perdures in the continued existing of the creature.

Compare what happens when a light is suddenly turned on in a darkened room. One can conceive of a first moment of light, but the activity involved in the continued illumination is exactly the same as in that first moment. So it is with creation. Its true essence does not lie in the notion of a beginning so much as in an assertion of an ongoing and dynamic ontological dependence on the Creator of the created universe, the first moment of which is the beginning of all beginnings.[4]

And again, if in a thought experiment you were to think of the sun as a limitless source of pure light, then the planets and the moon would be understood to *participate* or share in the sun's light by reason of its activity and according to the capacity of each to receive light. On this conception too, the sun plus its planets makes up more lighted things but not more light than does the sun alone. And the shared light of the moon and the planets is constantly and utterly dependent on the sun's radiation. Analogously, Aquinas considers that all finite beings exist only insofar as they are able to participate, each in its own way, in the unlimited source of existing, pure existential actuality—which is Aquinas's philosophic conception of God.

11.4 THE BIPOLARITY OF PARTICIPATED ACTS OF EXISTING

Though helpful in many ways, the above example of light leaves out, in my view, an essential aspect of the theory of participation in the act of existing, what I venture to call its "bipolarity."[5] For the act of participated existing is not unidirectional, simply received on the part of the participating being. It is at the same time intrinsically oriented back toward the Source of all existing, which is unlimited Existing Itself. (This obviously is the correlate of Plotinus's *return*.) This vector orientation to the Source of existing is not a mere adjunct to the theory of participation but part of its essence inasmuch as the infinite Source of existing is, in Aquinas's view, the root of all goodness and value, hence the ultimate goal of all existential activity.[6]

Furthermore, Aquinas could not have regarded this bipolar relationship as novel. It was, after all, implicitly contained in the commonly accepted medieval doctrine that Good is a "transcendental" aspect of Being in its natural attractiveness to the human will. Yet the importance of recognizing this inbuilt attraction back to the outflowing Source of Being can hardly be exaggerated for a fundamental ontology such as we are here attempting. It is the very core of teleology, the recognition of the role of final causality. That is why I have ventured to name this book simply *Aims*.

Chapter 12

Participation and God

12.1 PARTICIPATION AS A COSMOLOGICAL ARGUMENT FOR GOD

Arguments for the existence of God that begin with the experienced universe (cosmos) and then conclude to the existence of a supreme being that is the necessary cause of the existence of that cosmos or of some aspect of it have traditionally been called "cosmological" arguments. But the above rough description requires to be exactly understood. It does not primarily ask, "Is there a God?" Rather, it asks questions about the universe, namely, "What are the necessary conditions for the intelligibility of the given, existent universe? Is the universe self-explanatory in its existential givenness?" The argument evokes the insight that the intelligibility of the existing universe requires the continued causal influx of a source of that existing, and that such a source must exist by reason of itself, so that it exists necessarily. Thus the universe that we experience and find more or less intelligible is not self-explanatory but is intelligible only through an ongoing, causally dependent relationship on a unique being transcendent of the universe.[1]

Now Aquinas's core theory that all finite acts of existing flow by participation from a limitless source of existing is an intellectual vision both of the universe and of its relation to that source. It amounts to asserting that the universe is intelligible only by reason of its relation to that source. Hence to embrace Aquinas's theory of participation amounts to accepting its validity as an implicit argument for the actuality of that source of existing.

In Aquinas's "Five Ways" for arguing to God he concludes, respectively, (1) to an ultimate source of all motion or becoming, (2) to an ultimate cause of all causing, (3) to an ultimately necessary being, (4) to a source of all existential perfection (a kind of compact expression of the theory of participation), and (5) to an ultimate intelligence underlying the order of the universe.[2] In each case he adds: "And this is what everyone understands to be God." This latter step is of course quite a leap, but it is provisionally justified in the context both for brevity and in anticipation of later arguments. In this essay, however, I prefer, when possible, to avoid using the word "God" in the argument because of all the historical and religious overtones that the word naturally brings with it. In the theory of participation of existing one can speak of the source of existing without importing those other considerations. If it is not an unacceptable neologism, I propose sometimes to call that source "Alpha," and mean by it only what our above argument and conceptuality have implied.

It is a common experience that Aquinas's Fourth Way—by appeal to God as a source of participated existence—is initially the most obscure but in the end the most persuasive of his arguments. Since I have so far barely sketched his theory of participation, I can hardly suppose that the reader has already found it convincing as a fundamental philosophic perspective. I therefore think it useful to add a different way of arguing to an ultimate, transcendent source of existence that fits quite exactly what I have called Alpha in the Thomistic theory of participation. Thus, the two approaches may be seen to reinforce each other.

12.2 AN ARGUMENT FOR GOD AS THE NECESSARY SOURCE OF EXISTING

I begin with the following preliminary considerations.[3]

(1) There do exist some beings (*fact of experience*). Once again I assert that we observe extramental, corporeal things around us (rather than merely our own sensations). If one were a pure idealist, or even a solipsist, it would suffice for the argument that one admits that one's self, at least, exists.

(2) Beings cannot have arisen from sheer nothingness (*claim*). This is one way of putting Whitehead's "ontological principle." He writes: "According to the ontological principle there is nothing which floats into the world from nowhere. Everything in the actual world is referable to some actual entity [Whitehead's technical term for an ultimate existent, what I call a primary being]."[4]

(3) Hence there cannot have been a time when nothing whatever existed; (*conclusion*).[5] Consequently something (or other) has always existed.

From this alone it does not follow that some *single* being has always existed (as one might take Aquinas to mean in his Third Way), only that some beings or other were in existence at all "times." Thus there is the logical possibility, at least, that time never had a beginning and that there has been a past, endless (infinite) series of finite beings succeeding one another. (Such a series would be "horizontal" in the sense I suggested above.)

(4) All the beings of our experience are observed to be dependent for their act of existing on some other things, and that in two ways: for their coming into existence and for their remaining in existence (*fact of experience*). Beings that are

thus dependent on other beings (in either way) are called *contingent* beings.

With these preliminary considerations in mind, we are in a position to ask the following question.

(5) Is it rationally conceivable that absolutely *every* being is contingent, that is, dependent on some other being for its existing?

(6) Answer (*conclusion*): No, it cannot be that every being has its sufficient reason for existing in some other being, for this would violate the ontological principle (2). It would amount to asserting that there is no sufficient reason for the existence of the whole ensemble of contingent things.

For even if, as was mentioned under (3), there were an infinite temporal series of contingent events, such that the sufficient reason for any particular being could always be found in the previous beings, there would still be no sufficient reason for the whole sequence of contingent things. The whole universe would lack a sufficient reason for existing, and would thus be intrinsically unintelligible.

(7) The conclusion to which we are forced is that there must exist at least one being that is its *own* adequate reason for existing. As such, it cannot possibly not exist; it is a necessary being.[6]

As I have framed it, this argument roughly mirrors that developed by Leibniz in his essay, "On the Ultimate Origination of Things." There he sums it up as follows: "Since the ultimate ground [for the universe] must be in something which is of metaphysical necessity, and since the reason for an existing thing must come from something that actually exists, it follows that there must exist some one entity of metaphysical necessity, that is, there must be an entity whose essence is existence, and therefore something must exist which differs from the plurality of things, which differs from the world, which we have granted and shown is not of metaphysical necessity."[7]

Notice that this is not to say that that necessary entity (or any entity, for that matter) *causes* its own existence. As the word is used, a cause stands ontologically prior to its effect. It would therefore be incoherent to suppose that any being whatever (even God) could cause itself to exist. For it would ontologically have to exist if it is to exercise causality, but that is absurd if the required effect is its own very existing. It is another matter altogether, however, to think that some being might be its own *sufficient reason* for existing. It would simply exist because, so to speak, it can't help but exist. It does not come before itself in any way, it simply *is* itself, atemporally, inexorably, and by reason of itself. It would be a *necessary* being.

(8) As its own sufficient reason for existing, the necessary being must be simply identified with the pure and limitless act of existing; it cannot exist only in some particular, finite way. Only as itself limitless can it serve as the ultimate source of participated existing for all other beings. Thus all its characteristics are those that we (and Aquinas) attributed to Alpha (or God). It is identical to the source of all participated existing.

Chapter 13

The Problem of the Origin of Essential Aims

We are now in a position to confront the long postponed problem of how essential aims may be thought to arise. On closer examination it appears that this is no ordinary problem, one among many others, but rather the keystone problem of the whole possibility of constructing a structured, teleological metaphysics. Let us then take a hard look at the exact problem as it now reveals itself in the light of the metaphysical perspective we have so far developed.

13.1 THE COMPONENTS OF THE PROBLEM

(1) The question at hand primarily concerns the very coming to be of any primary being. By our previous analysis of the hypothetical metaphysical structure of any primary being, it is clear that to inquire into the existential origin of a primary being is also to inquire into the ultimate principle that defines it in existence, its essential aim. Correlative with this, I confine

the present discussion to the basic act of existence of the primary being, its *esse,* not its activity.[1] I am not now asking the origin of a primary being's immediate aims for action. I ask here the reason why the being is the kind of being that it is, with its own self-ideal, not why it acts in pursuit of the particular goals that I have called immediate aims.[2] (2) Unlike Whitehead, I assume that primary beings, rather like Aristotle's *ousíai,* endure in time according to the nature of their essential aims, and that, in so doing, they change internally in various ways without losing their self-identity. I assume, in particular, that a human being is a single primary being over a lifetime, not a succession of distinct, momentary beings however closely associated. A consequence of this is that essential aim functions in my philosophic perspective in much the same way as does Aquinas's substantial form, if one takes essential aim as also determining what I call the essential character of the entity.

(3) I accept the "ontological principle" (section 3.4, principle iv) whereby the ultimate reason why anything is, or is such, must be found in one or more primary beings, for ultimate reasons do not arise out of nowhere.

(4) We have already seen (section 5.2) that the primary being cannot provide for itself its own essential aim; rather, that aim must be provided for it by another primary being or beings. We have to ask therefore whether that aim can somehow be given to the being from the primary beings of its own past world.

Certainly in the case of the coming to be of a primary being of a more sophisticated sort—such as in the evolutionary emergence of life, of sensibility, and of intelligence—the answer to that question seems to be no. For consider what is requisite for such an aim. It must on the one hand be compatible with the factual structure of the whole world—otherwise chaos and failure would be the result—and on the other hand it must introduce into the world an aim toward an attainable yet higher order of value experience, an order that has never yet been achieved. There is nothing given in the past world that instantiates that particular, novel possibility for value achievement. Yet the nascent primary being feels that possibility as an attractive aim.

I do not think that any sort of Darwinian natural selection is adequate to account wholly for the evolutionary emergence of higher orders of existing. I cannot, of course, provide a strict demonstration of the correctness of my view. Here we are, as often, in a situation beyond demonstration where a choice must be made according to its plausibility. Having rejected the adequacy of a purely evolutionary answer, I must seek some other way of accounting for the origin of novel value in the universe.

(5) I continue to assume the theory of the participated character of the act of existing from a single source of that existing, which I have called Alpha. It is therefore an obvious question whether Alpha is itself the origin of every essential aim. There are several reasons for thinking so. For Alpha is the source of the very coming into existence of the primary being whose act of existing is limited to a determinate manner of existing. To what can we attribute this determinateness?

We have noted that there are strict requisites for the definite character of any essential aim. It must on the one hand be compatible with the general character of the whole universe, otherwise it would be self-destructive, and on the other it must in many cases introduce genuine but compatible novelty into the universe. By the ontological principle, does not Alpha uniquely fill the bill for meeting these requirements? Let me spell this out more exactly.

What we require here, if there is to be coherent order and even novelty in the universe, is a *unique matrix of possibility* for such an order of interrelated primary beings. By the ontological principle it follows that the unique, universal order of possibility must reside in some single primary being. No finite primary being can ground this order of universal possibility, and neither would a collection of such beings, not even that of the whole given world, for all these beings would have to share the identical envisagement of what is existentially possible and what is not. But that is not only a far less plausible hypothesis than attributing this envisagement to a single being, it also leaves the ontological principle unsatisfied with respect to the whole.

(6) I have also maintained that every act of existing is *bipolar*, so that it tends back toward its source even as it is received from it. In the nature of things, therefore, Alpha could very well be called Alpha/Omega. *The particular way that any act of existing thus tends back to its source is itself the very character defined by essential aim.* So to impart to each nascent primary being its very act of existing is ipso facto also to give it its essential aim.

(7) We find, moreover, that both Aquinas and Whitehead attribute the universal order of possibility to a unique being. For Aquinas, it is God, the same God who is the Source of all participated existing. God, in knowing himself, thereby knows all the possible ways in which his own nature, which is Existing Itself, can be communicated.[3] This is God's knowledge of all the "possibles." In creating finite beings, God creates them according to the matrix of possibilities for existing that God thus recognizes within himself.

Whitehead does something quite analogous in recognizing a "primordial" nature in God that is exactly such an ordered envisagement of possibilities for value achievement in the world. He writes: "Viewed as primordial, he [God] is the unlimited conceptual realization of the absolute wealth of potentiality."[4] For Whitehead, God thus becomes the necessary foundation of both the coherence and the novelty arising in the world precisely by furnishing to each nascent primary being (which he calls an "actual entity" or "actual occasion [of experience]") the initial form of its "subjective aim" (what I call essential aim): "[God] is that actual entity from which each temporal concrescence receives that initial aim from which its self-causation starts."[5]

It will shed more light on the problem of the origin of aims if we consider in more detail Whitehead's extraordinary solution to it.

13.2 WHITEHEAD'S ACCOUNT OF THE ORIGIN OF INITIAL AIMS

Whitehead's conception of "initial aim" (the initial phase of a "subjective aim") is roughly identical to what I have called "essential aim," though his application of the notion is much more far-ranging than mine. By reason of Whitehead's event-atomism, his notion of subjective aim in effect comprises both what I have called essential aim and immediate aims. For Whitehead to attribute to God the origin of all subjective aims is to attribute to God a far more detailed governance of all events than I propose by attributing to Alpha all essential but not immediate aims, which I explained under (1) above.

As I described in more detail in *Coming To Be*,[6] Whitehead apparently conceives that God experiences (feels) the world-situation of every actual entity as it is about to come into being. That is, God (in his "consequent" nature) feels the factuality of the whole world of immediately past actual entities at that particular perspective. God thus feels the causal impact of all past actual entities as they impinge upon the nascent entity. At the same time God (in his "primordial" nature) also feels the available possibilities for value achievement inherent in that situation. Thus God feels and *feels for* the best that that new actual entity can make of itself. This is possible because God in his primordial nature simply *is* the total envisagement of all interrelated possibilities for value.

Finally—and here, it seems to me, is Whitehead's stroke of genius—the nascent entity, which for Whitehead is identical to its bundle of experiential feelings of both fact and possibility, feels or experiences God *in God's feelings for it*. But for the new entity to feel God's positive feelings for it as just described, is precisely for it to be furnished with its own initial aim, its finally determining aim at self-fulfillment. In this way Whitehead solves with one stroke the two problems of accounting for both the coherence (hence intelligibility) of the universe, and the irruption of enriching novelty into the world.

To what extent can we appropriate Whitehead's solution in our own metaphysics?

Chapter 14

Three Options
for a Solution

Given the problem as defined above, the following three types of solution seem naturally to present themselves:

14.1 A THOMISTIC-TYPE SOLUTION

I say "type" because the problem before us is not exactly a problem that faced Aquinas, and so his solution will not quite fit ours either. I have replaced Thomistic hylomorphism with another conceptuality that is partly adapted from Whitehead and in which the correlative concepts of what I have called essential aim and essential character in effect perform the functions of Aquinas's substantial form. Thus to ask the origin of the essential aim of a primary being is analogous, though not identical, to Aquinas's asking the origin of the substantial form of a substance.

The question immediately arises whether we are considering a primary being that is the first of its kind—the beginning of a species—or rather a being that is in some way reproduced from its antecedents. For Aquinas the chicken clearly has priority over the egg, and in his culture he may have supposed that the various familiar species of creatures were created right from the beginning, more or less in the way described in the book of Genesis. Thus God would himself have supplied the substantial forms of all creatures in the very act of first creating them. The only remaining question, then, was whether God was needed to supply the substantial forms of succeeding beings of the same species, as in plant and animal reproduction.[1]

Aquinas holds that God, as the ultimate cause, is active in every creature's activity. Thus he argues that it pertains to the perfection of the divine power that God is able to communicate to creatures, according to their nature, a share in his own causal power.[2] In particular, God gives to plants and animals the power themselves to generate offspring of their own kind. This means that in addition to providing the necessary biological ground, such as the semen received within the body of the mother, the substantial form of the father produces a like substantial form in the offspring through imparting to the semen a certain instrumental "active power" that operates in its stead. So he writes that in animal generation, "a kind of active power belonging to the animal or plant seed is derived from the soul of the generator, just as an instrument derives a kind of motive power from the principal agent. And just as it does not matter whether we say that something is moved by the instrument or by the principal agent, so also it does not matter if we say that the soul of the generated is caused by the soul of the generator or by a power in the semen derived from the latter."[3]

As to the evolutionary emergence of new and higher species—a phenomenon not recognized in Aquinas's day—it is hard to see how Thomistic hylomorphism could deal with this unless, as at the first creation, God himself provides, at the arising of each novel and higher-level living substance, an appropriate new and higher substantial form.

How might we adapt Aquinas's solution to his problem to our own? We would have to say that in the case of ordinary animal or plant reproduction within the same species, the generating plants or animals provide to the newly forming offspring (a primary being) its essential aim. They give it its specific orientation to Alpha, the source of existing, and thus provide it with its unifying essential character and its principle of activity. That essential aim needs to be a feeling for a possible but as yet unrealized achievement of existing, and it needs to be consonant with the conditions and limitations laid upon the new primary being by its own past. The key question here seems to be how one or more finite primary beings may be thought to furnish, on their own, this ideal for the future to their successors. This seems perplexing though not unthinkable. But in the case of the emergence of higher order beings, it does seem unthinkable both for Aquinas, without the operation of God, and for our perspective, without the activity of Alpha. Just how such special activity of Alpha might be conceived will be examined in the next chapter.

14.1.1 Comments on the Thomistic-Type Solution

That a special intervention of Alpha is required to supply the essential aims of new and higher types of primary beings, such as in the origins of life, of sentience, and of intelligence, seems necessitated in a Thomistic-type solution to our problem. But it may be that, even in the more ordinary case of natural generation within a species, the Thomistic hylomorphic explanation of generation is not without its difficulties. Consider again the generation of a rabbit. Neither the sperm nor the egg is actually a rabbit, though the two properly united have the *potentiality* for the actuality of the substantial form of a rabbit. Now no one questions that rabbits generate rabbits, and so Aquinas affirmed that the substantial form that actualizes each of the parents produces, by means of its power imparted to the semen, a similar substantial form in the offspring.

Just how do the parents manage this? Of course they provide the appropriate material elements, namely the fertilized egg. But even for Aquinas that fertilized egg is not a new rabbit absent the dynamic, unifying, active principle that is the substantial form or soul. The egg constitutes only a proximate potentiality for the actuality of the new, dynamic substantial form, a principle of being, not itself material, and not identical to the material elements of the rabbit. Yet only through those elements can the parents act, and so Aquinas posits an "active power" (*vis activa*) imparted to the semen by the soul of the male parent, which power acts instrumentally for the parent in producing a like soul in the offspring.

Is this the only way in which we can reasonably account for the autonomous activity of creatures? Is it even the best way? Consider the new procedure of generating zygotes, even human zygotes, in a laboratory petri dish. Neither the sperm nor the egg is itself a human being nor, consequently, is it animated, in Thomas's conceptuality, by a human substantial form. Yet their union does sometimes unquestionably produce new human life. But the contributing parents not only need not be present, they may both be long since dead and it makes no difference to the process. How are we reasonably to think of the substantial forms of the parents, which by Aquinas's doctrine are the chief principles at work here, as nevertheless operative in absentia? Doesn't this sound rather like magic?

Another possible difficulty with Aquinas's theory may arise from his doctrine (and that of Roman Catholic theology) that the human soul cannot itself have emerged simply through a biological evolutionary process but is immediately created by God, inasmuch as it is manifestly ordered to activities that transcend the limitations of matter.

With Aquinas I accept that position, but I wonder what it says about his hylomorphic analysis of human generation. Both human parents are animated by souls that already transcend the capacities of materiality. I take the point about the necessity of God's activity to produce a soul transcendent of matter, but here we already have two such transcendent souls carrying out their inbuilt natural drive toward procreation. Since that is the case, then if Aquinas's theory that a soul by its power generates a like soul in its offspring, why should human souls not be able to exercise this natural ability to produce on their own a like transcendent soul in their offspring? That at least seems to be a difficulty.

14.2 A WHITEHEADIAN-TYPE SOLUTION

Once again I qualify this solution with the word "type" since we are not here working entirely within the Whiteheadian conceptual framework, and the possible solution to be examined here is in an important sense simpler than would be called for in Whitehead's conceptuality.

Whitehead judged that in order to account for both the stability and the emergent novelties in the universe, the initial aim for every actual entity must be provided by a unique actual entity that is in some senses infinite and that he calls "God." At the same time Whitehead maintained that his metaphysical ultimates (his actual entities) do not themselves change, they only *become,* and each instance of such becoming was thought to occur in a very small measure of time—perhaps, for a human being, as short as a tenth of a second. Because of his several metaphysical presuppositions, including a mistaken conception of how Aristotle conceived "substance,"[4] Whitehead could not allow that any of his actual entities perdure through any larger interval of time. Thus he was compelled to think of a human being, say, as consisting of a tightly ordered historical sequence of ontically discrete and temporally minute actual entities, each of which requires from God an infused "initial aim"—the initial stage of what I have called "essential aim." Most importantly, Whitehead seems systematically unable to distinguish, as I do, between the essential aim, which constitutes a primary being, and lesser, immediate aims successively chosen by that same primary being as conducive to its essential aim. For he equates change not with a process taking place within an actual entity but with the difference between two succeeding actual entities.[5] Thus every decision, however trivial, must be part of the constitution of a new actual entity, and so be a function of a new subjective aim (Whitehead's term that most nearly equates with what I call essential aim).

This contrasts strongly with the metaphysical solution (14.2) under consideration here, in which an animal, or a human person, is conceived to be a single primary being over the course of its lifetime and in virtue of its unique essential aim. Thus I require only that Alpha furnish once to each primary being its particular essential aim, whereas Whitehead in effect requires that Alpha furnish all the additional, subordinate aims (what I have called immediate aims) that, in my view, the selfsame primary being is able to adopt for itself in view of its essential aim.

Three things may be noticed. First of all, the solution being considered here (14.2) concerns the furnishing of the *final* cause, the ultimate aim, to the primary being in its coming to be. It does not directly involve *effective* causes. Alpha is not conceived as taking over the machinery of the universe. Secondly, final causality requires essential reference to the *universal order of possibility* that by the ontological principle must be thought to reside in Alpha. Thirdly, by the bipolar nature of participated existing, Alpha's very act of furnishing to each nascent primary being its own act of existing at the same time orders the primary being back to Alpha/Omega Itself, and does it in the particular way that is coherent with the possibility for value that is available for that being.[6] Thus the more primitive sorts of primary beings would naturally be conceived as ordered to an existence of dull, unimaginative repetition of the past, whereas the more sophisticated kinds of beings would be the created well-springs of novel achievement of value.[7]

14.2.1 Comments on the Whiteheadian-Type Solution

Whitehead himself once said, on hearing a complex metaphysical position expounded by a young scholar, "Reality cannot be half so complicated!"[8] It seems to me that his remark applies eminently to his own position regarding the furnishing of subjective aims. Can we seriously imagine that Alpha must provide the goal for every event in the universe, however trivial? Even if we could, does not such a view amount to a kind of occasionalism in which God does everything and nature does nothing? And would not such a nature, constantly guided by Alpha's knowledge of possibilities, be far more harmonious than we observe it to be? Similar difficulties might be brought against the more modified Whiteheadian-type solution considered below. Yet it must be admitted that such a solution does reply to the problem of accounting for essential aims, especially novel ones, even at what may appear to be an exorbitant cost.

14.3 A MORE MODIFIED WHITEHEADIAN-TYPE SOLUTION

Perhaps we could envision a kind of compromise between a Thomistic-type solution and the Whiteheadian-type just sketched, in which Alpha's special activity is required only for the provision of novel or higher-order essential aims, but not for repeating already existent sorts of aims, such as occur in animal or plant generation. Thus Alpha would solve the problem of evolutionary advance, but primary beings themselves could seem to account for their own natural activity such as procreation. As in the Thomistic-type solution, Alpha is needed to account for the emergence of higher order beings but not for the perpetuation of species.

14.3.1 Comments on the More Modified Whiteheadian-Type Solution

This at first may seem a happy compromise, but the plot thickens when one tries to spell it out more exactly. For instance, what precisely constitutes a "higher order" as well as a "novel" essential aim? Perhaps this difficulty is only symptomatic of the weakness of the human imagination, but it does seem mind-boggling to try to distinguish just wherein a new and greater order of value orientation would consist. It all begins to seem quite arbitrary and even to add complication rather than simplicity to an already complex problem. Apparently it is a fact that some evolutionary advances are barely incremental rather than dramatically novel. Is there a line to be drawn here? If this is indeed the right direction of a solution, it seems a murky one at best.

It also shares the difficulty mentioned above in criticism of the Thomistic-type solution. Getting back to the proliferating rabbits, the parents in their activity produce a suitable union of sperm and egg. This biological product has—or even *is*—a proximate potentiality for the actuality of Thomas's substantial form or my essential aim and essential character. But they are not themselves that actuality. It requires an appropriate agent in actuality (the ontological principle again) to raise that potentiality to a state of actuality. The most obvious such agents are the generating parents, and Aquinas is satisfied with them as providing that agency.

But the agency of providing the necessary biological combination is one activity, that of providing the substantial form or the essential aim is another. One should resist the temptation to become bewitched by the obvious *fact* of generation when the real problem is to account for it. Can a Thomistic-type solution do that adequately? It may sound satisfying to say that the substantial form of the parents produces, all on its own, a new, distinct substantial form in the offspring, and it is unquestionable that such a form does arise. But what is the best explanation of this "production"? I have proposed the three possibilities that occur to me. (There may of course be more.) If we have to choose from among them, which is the most plausible choice?

Chapter 15

Making a Choice

15.1 EXPANSION OF THE PROPOSED SOLUTION

William James advised that when certitude is not attainable—as it seldom is in philosophy—the most reasonable position to take is the one that is the most intellectually satisfying.[1] I think he did not mean the most comfortable, an intellectual old shoe, but the most revealing, even perhaps the most exciting. And I note that the late Thomas Gold, astronomer and highly original cosmologist, is reported to have said, "In choosing a hypothesis, there isn't any virtue in being timid."

All things considered, then, I judge that what I have termed the "Whiteheadian-type solution" is the most intellectually satisfying of the three options.[2] Permit me to set it once again in context, and to expand on it for the sake of clarity and to show its plausibility. Finally, I shall endeavor to meet objections against it.

As I mentioned in section 13.2, Whitehead is usually understood to have the nascent actual entity *feel God in God's feelings for it*. That, I think, is a profound idea, but can it be given an interpretation analogously appropriate to the perspective I am here trying to work out? I essay the following.

First, we are not dealing here with the experiences of an already constituted primary being but with that very constitution itself. (Recall from section 13.1 the restriction of the discussion to *esse,* the primary being's "first act.") This first act of existing is not an experience in the ordinary sense of the word, let alone is it a "feeling." It does however have what I have called an essential character, the natural correlate to its essential aim. It is filtered, so to speak, by that aim.

Second, the nascent primary being does not arise in a vacuum but out of a particular past world of factuality. That world lays the conditions of possibility for value realization in the future. Now Whitehead conceives that what he calls God, in his "consequent nature," feels (experiences) that same world out of which the new primary being arises. I think that Aquinas too would basically agree with this (at least if we take "feels" simply in the sense of "is aware of, including its value dimension"), inasmuch as he argues that since the cause is simultaneous with its effect, and since God, as the primary cause, is at work in every causal event, God is in that sense everywhere.[3] Whitehead's God at the same time and by reason of his "primordial nature," feels the spectrum of possibilities for experiential value achievement for that nascent being, and thereby feels *for*—inclines toward—the better possibilities. If one then supposes, as Whitehead apparently does, that the newly forming being *feels God's feelings for it and its own future,* then that is identical with the being itself being provided with its essential aim (Whitehead's "initial aim"), the feeling for its own self-ideal aiming at the immediate future.[4]

I think it would be possible to save the essence of this idea without introducing a Thomistically unacceptable activity of the world upon God or of the primary being's literally feeling God. For I can conceive Alpha as being experientially aware of the nascent being's situation in the world, together with Alpha's recognition of the entire matrix of value possibilities in their interrelations. Since Alpha's aim in the world is value achievement (a concept shared by both Aquinas and Whitehead), it is plausible that Alpha would furnish to each newly forming primary being an attraction (essential aim) toward that particular way of existing in which it would be most existentially enriched. Such an attraction is *a way of receiving participated existing* and forms a necessary aspect of Alpha's furnishing existence (*esse*) to the being. Since Alpha (like Aquinas's "God") alone is the source of existing, Alpha must furnish to every primary being its act of existing. But such an act of existing is necessarily limited to existing in just this way or that, so that Alpha's providing the primary being with its essential aim is simply an aspect of Alpha's creative act for it. Alpha orients the created primary being back to itself (Alpha is Omega as well) in just that particular way that defines the primary being.

In the end, then, I propose (1) *that Alpha creates the essential aim for every primary being,* and (2) *does it in a way that is compatible with Aquinas's conception of creation and his theory of participation.* But what exactly are the differences between my view and those of Whitehead and of Aquinas?

I differ from Whitehead by attending more explicitly to the act of existing as flowing forth from God through participation.[5] And since I allow my primary beings to endure through sometimes considerable spans of time, I require far fewer provisions of essential aims than Whitehead does for his more numerous actual entities.

I differ from Aquinas in replacing his Aristotelian notion of substantial form with a notion of essential aim taken together with its correspondent essential character. I discard Aristotelian/Thomistic hylomorphism in favor of what I consider to be a more dynamic concept of the unity of a primary being.

In line with this, I abandon the Thomistic hylomorphic doctrine that in natural generation the parents themselves existentially produce the substantial form of the offspring. In general I do not see how substantial forms — or my essential aims — can be generated except by bringing God (or Alpha) into the causal activity. This of course contravenes Aquinas's explicit statements,[6] yet I maintain that Aquinas would have been more consistent with his own deeper metaphysical principles had he abandoned speaking here in borrowed hylomorphic language. For in the coming to be of the new offspring, neither it nor its substantial form preexisted its coming into being. There is a nontemporal simultaneity of the coming into existence of both the being and its substantial form. The parents, in this case, make available the bodily configuration suitable to the emergence and functioning of such a substantial form. But that configuration is not identical with the form itself; it is only a potentiality and a necessary condition for that form. Does it not make more sense in the light of Aquinas's wider thought to say that on the occasion of the provision by the parents of the bodily configuration (or proximate potentiality) for the functioning of such a form, God, in his wider wisdom, renders that form actual by the very act of sharing his existing in that particular way? But then is this not to say that God creates all substantial forms — or in my language, all essential aims?

I take it that the central point of contention here lies not in Alpha's providing truly novel and higher-order essential aims, as in evolutionary advance to higher forms, but in the claim that such activity of Alpha is requisite for the production of the essential aim of each and every finite primary being whether of a novel sort or not. That this, however, seems a reasonable explanation may appear from the following considerations.

(a) We have seen — as just above — the difficulty of attributing the origin of the immediate aim to the antecedent primary beings, as for instance in animal generation. This solution removes that difficulty.

(b) We are dealing here with final, not with effective, causality. Alpha is conceived simply as giving a certain existential orientation of the nascent primary being back to its source—which is what I have suggested we can call Alpha/Omega. Such an orientation exactly constitutes a final cause.

(c) To put this more explicitly into our accepted context of the participation of the act of existing: Alpha gives to each being, both in its coming to be and in its continued duration, its very act of existing. That is an instance of effective causality on the part of Alpha. But concomitantly with the effective sharing out of existence, Alpha necessarily imparts to that act of existing an orientation back to Itself. This explicitates what I have called the *bipolarity* of the act of existing: its dual aspect of both flowing forth from and tending back to its Source.[7]

(d) Such an imparted orientation would be specific, not just generic. This assertion fits both Aquinas's conception that specific Divine Ideas stand as the patterns employed by God in creating, and Whitehead's conception that God adjusts his giving of initial aims to the specific ordering of all possibilities for value that constitutes God's primordial nature.

(e) I keep in mind, and agree with, Aquinas's conviction that both God and natural agents can and do cooperate in producing a single effect, so that the total effect is ascribable both to God and to the creature but to each in a different way.[8] In the case of natural procreation, the parents effectively produce the appropriate biological configuration, with its aptitude for fulfilling a certain essential aim, but I conceive that Alpha concomitantly imparts to the offspring both its act of existing and, according to the aptitude of that biological configuration, its inbuilt particular orientation back to its Source. The proper biological configuration (say, the sperm and the egg with necessary attendant circumstances) constitutes the necessary condition for, but is not identical with, the orientation toward existence that is the essential aim, analogously to the way Aquinas regarded the proper disposition of the body as required for, but not identical with, its substantial form or soul. As to the orientation of the act of existing back to its Source, there is no separating that act of existing from its orientation, and that orientation just *is* the essential aim of the primary being.

I suggest, then, that the Whiteheadian-type account of the origin of essential aims, as just described, is the most plausible of the three options. In that view Alpha provides for each and every primary being the essential aim that governs the being's nature and activities for as long as it perdures.

Against the background of this more detailed exposition of the suggested solution, let us now take a hard look at the objections that can be posed against that view. Facing them will itself further illuminate the position.

15.2 OBJECTIONS AND REPLIES

15.2.1 Objection 1: You Cannot Be Serious! or: Ockham's Razor Swipes Again

This objection appeals to the apparent absurdity of the proposed solution—though I recall the observation of David Lewis that "one man's reason is another man's *reductio.*"[9] As was remarked in the previous chapter, can we seriously suppose that God is a kind of cosmic busybody involved in the origin of every ant or of every newly formed atom of helium in the sun? Such a view seems to strain belief beyond belief. In fact, it seems a clear case of a philosophic *deus ex machina,* a contrived, *ad hoc,* and implausible solution invoked in desperation.

Reply

I submit, first of all, that it must be at least possible that this solution, bizarre as it may at first sound, simply results from taking seriously the fundamental idea that the universe is goal-oriented, teleological. I earlier quoted Etienne Gilson as saying: "Philosophers are free to lay down their own sets of principles, but once this is done, they no longer think as they wish—they think as they can."[10] Now, in supporting principle vi of section 3.4, I argued that all basic activities within nature are goal-directed, aiming at some further fulfillment, although usually not consciously so. What then is really entailed in supposing that all process is goal-oriented? The answer comes as a shock. We are culturally so unused to thinking in terms of final causes that taking them seriously in their consequences appears at first outlandish.

Second, if, as Aquinas held, each and every primary being is intimately indebted to God for its very existence and causal power, why not also for its essential aim?

Third, I have given good reasons for thinking that the feeling of value is a universal experience. And, indeed, Aquinas holds that every being is ordered back to God as to the ultimate source of value. But the feeling of aims is just the feeling of the value of a possibility to be fulfilled for the primary being. The ontological principle requires that this relationship be grounded in an actual entity. The only open question is, where does this value relation of the primary being to an unfulfilled possibility reside? If, as I have also argued, the primary being cannot originate its own essential aim, then in what being is this relationship found? And would not the feeling of participated value be itself both a feeling of the source of that value (Alpha) and of an orientation back toward that source (a feeling of essential aim)? Why, then, should this solution be unthinkable?

Further, the Thomistic theory of the participation of the act of existing (*esse*)—which theory I accept—itself involves God in the origin of every ant or every atom of helium (if atoms in fact qualify as primary beings). For God is required to give and maintain for each primary being its act of existing. The proposition that God imparts to each primary being its own immediate aim simply specifies one factor in *how* God does this.

In Aquinas's analysis the "substantial form," which in a living being is called its "soul," plays a dual role. As the ultimate organizing principle of the being's (say, the rabbit's) body, the soul is a principle of fulfillment or actualization in the order of essence or whatness. Thus the soul of an animal relates to its body as actuality to potentiality. But in thus unifying the body toward its specific operation, the soul constitutes the body's capacity or potentiality for the act of existing in its own specific way, and this particularized act of existing is identical with the animal's *living,* according to the Scholastic adage, "For a living being, living *is* existing." So the soul is the animal's principle of actuality in the order of essence, and its principle of potentiality in the order of existence.

That, I believe, is the standard Thomistic analysis. Supposing that description is roughly correct, I notice in it the unavoidable implication that the key to the whole process is goal-directedness or teleology. The soul is acknowledged to act within the animal as its formal, effective, and final principle or cause: the soul makes the body to be the *sort* of body that it is, it is the driving principle within the animal of its specific activities, and it *orders the animal toward its own fulfillment.* In Aquinas's view this last is just to say that the soul orders the animal toward its appropriate Divine Idea through all the animal's activities.

Also, the animal for Aquinas is a single substance of which the unifying principle is the soul. The implication is that the soul unifies the body in its activities precisely by ordering it to its single proper end. Thus in the activity of animal procreation one must think of the soul as itself coming into existence exactly when the new animal does, for the very good reason that the soul is itself an essential principle of that coming to be. Now the body is not ordered to its unifying end simply in virtue of its physical characteristics. Rather, given those characteristics as necessary conditions, the body is a capacity or potentiality for that unifying ordering to its end provided by the soul. If therefore the body itself, in the order of essence, is only potentiality with respect to the soul which is its actuality, the question naturally arises, what provides that actuality for the body? Roughly, where does the soul come from, or better, how is it that the body, which is itself only a capacity for unity and goal-directedness, is given its unity and its orientation? And that is just the question at issue here.

When we transform the above Thomistic account into the metaphysical concepts that I am suggesting in this study, the question becomes, what provides the nascent animal with its essential aim? For the essential aim gives the primary being both its directedness toward an aim and governs its essential character and its activities. Yet, as we have seen, no finite primary being can furnish for itself its own essential aim.

Now since I already grant, with Aquinas, that God (Alpha) is the sole source of the act of existing for that new primary being, the question simply becomes, what gives to the act of existing of that primary being its very specific and particular orientation back to God? Is it not reasonable to think that Alpha, who is aware of all possibilities for value and their respective relationships (just as Aquinas thinks of God as creating according to his divine ideas), should orient each gift of participated existence back to itself in the way most suitable for the given biological configuration? But that orientation in existing is exactly the essential aim of the nascent primary being. What is extravagant about that?

In summary: for the parents effectively to produce the biological configuration (the fertilized egg) for their offspring is for them to produce a proximate potentiality for the life-giving principle (soul, or essential aim) of the offspring. But that biological configuration is only a potentiality for, not the actuality of, that principle. The question remains, what actualizes that potentiality? I suggest that Alpha Itself (speaking just philosophically) actualizes that potentiality precisely by suffusing the offspring not only with an act of existing but, concomitantly, by giving that act its particular orientation back to Alpha. This is exactly to furnish that act with its essential aim (or substantial form).

Ockham's razor is meant to cut away principles that are unnecessary. But the whole question here is whether God's provision of essential aims is in fact necessary. To this sort of metaphysical problem we cannot expect an unquestionable solution, but we are entitled to be content with the most plausible one. It seems to me we have that in the unique activity of Alpha.

15.2.2 Objection 2: The Solution Denies to the Beings of Nature Their Proper Activities

I confess that in *Coming To Be* I too closely identified essential aim with the essential character that is derivative from it, and thus gave some grounds for the impression that I deny to animals and plants the natural ability to generate their own offspring.[11] Thus, in a review of *Coming To Be,* professor W. Norris Clarke wrote:

> [In Felt's view] the whole constitutive structure (nature) of each new actual entity is now directly and immediately— and freely—infused by God, not passed on from the preceding perishing entities. But this taking over of the constitution of new natures almost entirely by God ends up by radically diminishing, if not effectively eliminating, the whole active generative causality of created beings, especially living beings, as passing on their own specific natures to their offspring. . . . What Felt is proposing effectively reduces the efficient causality of creatured [*sic*] natures into little more than material causality.[12]

Reply
Perhaps Clarke would not frame this objection so strongly against my position in the present book, but his objection is worth meeting in any case. Now, as I said before, I do not conceive God as taking over the machinery of the universe; I am not dealing with effective causality at all. I am not requiring God to substitute for the biological efficient causality of the parents. For God—or Alpha—to supply *goal orientation* to

the act of existing of a primary being is hardly for Alpha to supplant the effective, causal activity of the parents, which is actively to provide the biological proximate potentiality for the life of the offspring. But the whole question at issue here is: What is the origin or cause of the essential aim, the goal orientation, of the offspring? What brings the fertilized egg's potentiality for a life-giving substantial form (or essential aim) into actuality? In the previous chapter I offered (section 14.1.1) what I think are plausible reasons for doubting that it can simply be the biological parents who, it seems to me, have done all they can do in providing the fertilized egg.

Rather than reducing the effective causality of created natures into little more than material causality, my description requires that the parents effectively produce a very specific structure on the part of the offspring if it is to be suitable for the essential aim (or substantial form) of the offspring. That structure is a necessary condition, but still only a potentiality, for the actuality of the aim or form; it is not the actuality itself. And so we are back again to the original question of the source of that actuality.

In this context it is easy subconsciously to beg the question, and I fear that Clarke did just that when he also wrote in that review: "It seems undeniable that our whole experience of living beings reveals that, in fact, they pass on their own living forms to their offspring." He took that as corroboration of the Thomistic account of how a substantial form in the offspring is produced by the influence of the substantial form of the male parent. But this undeniable replication in the offspring of the same specific form is precisely what requires explanation, and the point at issue here is which explanation is the most plausible. Clarke appears to identify observable "passing on," in the sense of observable replication of a similar being, with the theoretic explanation of this replication that is given by the Thomistic, hylomorphic theory. He seems to suppose that the evident fact of reproduction itself proves the correctness of that theory. But the hylomorphic theory, like any other theory, cannot itself be observed, it is only one way of accounting for what does get observed. The question remains, is it the best way?

Finally, since Clarke rightly considers himself to be a Thomist-inspired philosopher, it is not impertinent to point out that my proposal that God or Alpha supplies to every nascent primary being its essential aim seems to me more in line with Aquinas's view than is the position implied by Clarke in his remarks quoted above. If I am not mistaken, Clarke's position might be paralleled as follows:

> Whenever God fashions a nature, by that very fact he gives it all that belongs essentially to it. Thus by the very fact that he makes a man he gives him a rational soul. Therefore by implanting natural forces in things, he enabled them to perform their natural operations. Hence there is no need for him [God] also to operate in nature.

Well, as the reader may have already recognized, I have just quoted from the fifth objection that Aquinas posed to himself when inquiring, in his *Disputed Questions on the Power of God*, "Does God work in operations of nature?"[13] To that question Aquinas replies: "I answer that we must admit without any qualification that God operates in the operations of nature and will."[14] In the course of his ensuing treatment Aquinas makes the following statements pertinent to our purpose:

> This or that individual thing *cannot by its action produce another individual of the same species except as the instrument of that cause* which includes in its scope the whole species and, besides, the whole being of the inferior creature [which cause, for Aquinas, is of course God]. . . .
>
> If, then, we consider the subsistent agent, every particular agent is immediate to its effect: but if we consider

the power whereby the action is done, then the power of the higher cause is more immediate to the effect than the power of the lower cause; since the power of the lower cause is not coupled with its effect save by the power of the higher cause. . . .

. . . Accordingly the divine power must needs be present to every acting thing, even as the power of the heavenly body must needs be present to every acting elemental body.[15]

It is significant that Aquinas likens God's causal activity here to that of the heavenly bodies acting on earthly ones. For in his Aristotelian-Ptolemaic cosmology, the heavenly bodies act on earthly ones precisely as final causes, as the objects of "desire." And that is analogously the sort of activity I am imputing to Alpha in furnishing the required essential aims. Also, in the *Summa Theologiae* Aquinas does not hesitate to invoke "a kind of heat derived from the power of the heavenly bodies" as requisite for explaining the "vital spirit" (*virtus animae*) in the semen "by virtue of which the lower agencies also act so as to produce the species."[16] If it is acceptable to think that the final and efficient influence of the heavenly bodies is requisite for animal generation, why should the activity of Alpha in supplying final causes be thought to derogate from the activities of nature?

Again, in summing up his argument before turning to the objections, Aquinas writes:

Therefore God is the cause of everything's action inasmuch as he gives everything the power to act, and preserves it in being and applies it to action, and inasmuch as by his power every other power acts. And if we add to this that God is his own power, . . . we shall conclude that he acts in every agent immediately, *without prejudice to the action of the will and of nature.*[17]

Finally, as part of his reply to the seventh objection Aquinas writes:

> It is possible for a natural thing to be given its own proper power as a permanent form within it, *but not the power to act so as to cause being as the instrument of the first cause,* unless it were given to be the universal principle of being. Nor could it be given a natural power to cause its own movement, or to preserve its own being. Consequently just as it clearly cannot be given to the craftsman's instrument to work unless it be moved by him, so neither can it be given to a natural thing to operate without the divine operation.[18]

I propose that one way of describing this divine operation is precisely that Alpha gives to each newly forming primary being its essential aim.

It is worth noticing too that in the pivotal chapter in his *On the Truth of the Catholic Faith,* in which Aquinas defends the proper activities of natural things from those who would deny them,[19] what Aquinas is explicitly aiming at is to refute the position of extreme occasionalists who deny to natural substances *any effective activity whatever.* That is hardly the position I am suggesting here. Also, that same chapter 69 is immediately preceded both by chapter 67, "That God Is the Cause of Operation for All Things that Operate," and by chapter 68, "That God Is Everywhere" [precisely because he "moves all things to their operations"], as well as followed by chapter 70, "How the Same Effect Is from God and from a Natural Agent."

15.2.3 Objection 3: The Scent of Occasionalism

One might object that the author's proposed Whiteheadian-type solution must be rejected as lapsing into the old, discredited doctrine of occasionalism in which all activity is attributed to God and none to creatures.

Reply

The objection is misplaced. Occasionalism in effect attributes to God all effective causality. My position, however, says nothing about effective causality but is wholly concerned with the origin of aims, with final causality. It was already established that the nascent primary being cannot produce or even choose its own essential aim. Alpha, in making available to the nascent primary being its own essential aim, contributes to it its finality, its *telos,* but does not supplant the producing of those conditions that are a necessary condition for the arising of the new primary being. Yet in the absence of its aim, the being would be unable to be or to act at all. The counterposition to this, that God's activity is not needed for the emergence of new essential aims (as in Clarke's conception of the hylomorphic theory of procreation) may seem to smack of a Deism in which God is conceived as unnecessary for the continued functioning of nature once it is created. Yet it is genuine Thomistic doctrine that all causal activity on the part of creatures takes place only through participating in the causal power of God.[20] In the solution that I accept, the processes of nature, including the emergence of new primary beings, participate in Alpha's aims as well as in Alpha's effective power.

15.2.4 Objection 4: Then Why So Many Failures?

The solution is highly implausible inasmuch as, if it is correct that Alpha provides all essential aims, the evolutionary history of nature should be smoother and more successful than we observe it to be. Why have there been so many evolutionary failures if Alpha engineers all the species through their essential aims?

Reply

The substance of this objection was originally made to me in conversation by Professor Clarke, and was repeated by him toward the end of his aforemonetioned review of *Coming To Be.*

I find it perhaps the most difficult objection of all. Certainly it cannot be easily dismissed. Without pretending, then, that the following two considerations are conclusive, I offer them as mitigating, at least, the force of the objection.

First, the objection hinges on a highly speculative guess, from our limited point of view, as to how the universal processes of nature should be expected to act in some hypothetical situation. "Would be" or "should be" judgments are always precarious, and to suppose that one knows what *would be* or *should be* the result of God's provision of all essential aims in the universe is surely to strain surmise to the limit.

Second, the main reply to the objection would seem to be found in the mystery of freedom. With Whitehead I accept that there may be at least some degree of freedom—self-origination and lack of constraint in action—in all primary beings. This is entailed in supposing a teleological universe in which final causes cause by attraction, not by necessitation, and so there is always the possibility, or even a probability, of a failure fully to realize in deed the ideal possibility presented by the essential aim. More in particular, I have distinguished between essential aim and the immediate aims that the primary being develops in view of the essential aim. But the development of immediate aims truly suitable for contributing to the essential aim is a fallible process attributable to the finite primary being, not to Alpha. Compare Aristotle's (and Aquinas's) distinction between happiness as the ultimate aim, and the choice of physical pleasure or fame or contemplation as means (I would say immediate aims) to achieve it. The alternative to a teleological, hence chancy, worldview is mechanism, and that is out of the question here.

Given all the above, I suggest that the attractiveness of the origin of essential aims proposed above outweighs the objections that I have seen brought against it. Indeed, I think that Whitehead's conception of how God actively provides each being with its aim, luring it to greater intensity of experience, is both illuminating and analogously consonant with Aquinas's own principles.

Aware that I am applying the text beyond Aquinas's immediate intention, I nevertheless close this chapter with the following line from his Fifth Way for demonstrating God in the *Summa Theologiae:* "Everything in nature, therefore, is directed to its goal by someone with understanding, and this we call God."[21]

Chapter 16

"Know Yourself!"

In Shakespeare's *Julius Caesar* Cassius says to Brutus: "Tell me, good Brutus, can you see your face?" "No, Cassius," replies Brutus, "for the eye sees not itself but by reflection, by some other things."[1] It might seem that this truism illustrates the difficulty of responding to the Delphic exhortation, "Know yourself!" But that wouldn't be right, since what can be seen in us from the outside is not what we are on the inside, and the Oracle challenges us to explore ourselves on the inside. To do this we must begin with exploring the character of our own immediate experience, for in a sense we *are* that experience, and in any case it points to *what* we are.

We have, in fact, been doing that kind of exploration throughout the previous chapters, and now we can make this more explicit. Our adopted metaphysical principles were drawn from reflection on immediate experience, and we want now to turn the resulting philosophic perspective back onto our experience to see whether it illuminates it by rendering it more intelligible.

Right away, however, a practical problem looms. How shall I phrase the following reflections? I cannot fairly write "you," since the object of these reflections is immediate experience and I cannot claim direct access to yours. For the same reason I cannot write "we," even though I have reason to suppose that we, as humans, have roughly the same basic experience. So I am forced to put things in terms of my own experience; to write "I" and "my," with the hope that you, the reader, will forgive this way of putting things, especially if, as I expect, your experience is very like my own.

This is, after all, not a novel way of writing philosophy. Perhaps we can think of the following reflections as a kind of Cartesian meditation. For though Descartes in his *Meditations on First Philosophy* claimed only to be recounting the sometimes tortuous path of his own inner reflections, he was patently not only inviting but confidently expecting the reader to be able to repeat those same experiences within the reader's own mind.

Glancing ahead, we see that our reflections will naturally fall into three stages: first, to summarize the earlier observational or phenomenological description we made of immediate experience; second, to frame a preliminary interpretation of that description in terms of general metaphysical principles; and third, to undertake a deeper analysis of the philosophic structure of ourselves and our experience in terms of the most fundamental metaphysical principles that we have here developed. This last stage will open up problems that, by a kind of philosophic Gödel's theorem, transcend philosophy itself.

16.1 A SHORT, PHENOMENOLOGICAL DESCRIPTION OF IMMEDIATE EXPERIENCE

What I first notice in my experiencing are *objects* in a *world*. These objects confront me sensibly as making a difference to me, for better or for worse. I may choose to ignore them, but I always do so at my own peril, for they give themselves to me as enjoying a certain autonomy of existence and activity.

Taken together they make up a *world* that I feel myself part of and that, in another sense, is a part of me.

Furthermore in finding myself confronted with these objects I also sense a dimension of *value* that belongs to them as I experience them. This sense of value, good or bad, attractive or harmful, is an ineluctable aspect of my experience of them.

I also find that I directly experience a sense of *derivation* of the present from the past, and of the present as issuing into a future. This is a feeling not only of subjective continuity but a feeling of the continuity through time of the experienced world itself.

Always present in my experiencing is a sense of my own unity: that although my body and my psyche are doubtless complex, yet they constitute a single, unitary me.

Another aspect of my experiencing might be called its stimulus-response dynamic. I literally feel the causal impact of the things that make up my world. They impose themselves upon me willy-nilly, and they call for a response on my part. In fact that seems to be the basic character of all my ordinary experience: an interactive, causal commerce with things in the world.

There is one such interaction, however, that is for me paramount: my relations with other human beings. There is no more concrete or valuable aspect of my experiencing than interpersonal relationships.

I also notice that all my deliberate acts are *aimed* acts: they are performed with the intention of achieving some as yet nonexistent value. And such value is not peripheral to me like clothing, but it is value-for-myself. Better: it is a kind of self-ideal, a new and better me that is aimed at in my every intentional action. Most importantly, underlying every such action is the lure of that central aim toward which all my particular aims focus, what I have called my essential aim. The trouble is, it is not immediately clear just what that aim is. As E. B. White wrote in a short story: "My heart has followed all my days something I cannot name."[2] Aristotle identified this ultimate aim as "happiness," by which he meant an activity of soul according to what is best in the soul, and that, he said, is intellectual contemplation.[3] That may at first sound too abstract, yet it does say something important.

16.2 PRELIMINARY PHILOSOPHICAL INTERPRETATION OF EXPERIENCING

My experiencing involves both the experienced objects and me the experiencer. I have satisfied myself that what I directly experience in sense perception is extramental objects themselves, not just my own sense data. Yet I do not experience objects as they are in themselves but as they stand related to me in my act of perceiving them. What I perceive are real but relational objects. Yet, precisely because they do act on me in my perception of them, I am entitled to attribute to them an existence in their own right. I thus have solid metaphysical grounds underlying my immediate feeling of being in a world of objects.

Also, my every act of experiencing is an activity in existence. I accept Aquinas's insight that the act of existing is the act of acts and is the root of all value. I take it that all my natural activities are a manifestation of the tendency of existing to overflow or communicate itself. The apex of such activity is found in interpersonal relationships.

As for myself, I take myself to be a primary being in the sense worked out earlier. I am individuated from other primary beings by my body. At the same time I am a highly complex being, containing within myself a myriad of subordinate entities. How then do I explain my sense of personal unity?[4] In terms of my overarching essential aim. Though my subordinate entities have particular aims of their own, yet, as part of me, their aims participate in my essential aim, so that my unity is dynamic and goal-aimed. I am one primary being because all of my parts share in my single essential aim.

I cannot myself have contrived or even chosen my essential aim, that of a human being; it must have been given to me from without. I have philosophically satisfied myself that just as my ongoing act of existing must continually be furnished to me and kept in actual existence by the Source of all existing that I call Alpha, so must my essential aim have been furnished to me and kept in existence by Alpha.[5] Also, the aim must have been precisely chosen so as to be conducive, in the fabric of things, to the realization of greater value.

It follows that the nature of my essential aim sets natural parameters for my life span. It must be at least theoretically possible for me to satisfy that essential aim through the particular activities that I engage in. My metaphysics, like Aquinas's but unlike Whitehead's, allows me to enjoy a real self-identity as a single primary being during all that time.

16.3 IN SEARCH OF ONE'S ESSENTIAL AIM

Again and again, then, I find that the central answer to the question, "What am I?" lies exactly in the nature of my essential aim.

I earlier distinguished my essential aim from what I call immediate aims, those particular, limited aims that I am constantly and explicitly adopting from moment to moment of my life. But they are all chosen only insofar as they are felt to conduce to my essential aim. One thinks of Aristotle who said that the ultimate aim underlying all other aims is happiness itself, so that particular aims are adopted just insofar as they are thought to contribute to happiness.

But, as I noticed earlier, my essential aim is too large, or rather too fundamental, to have been chosen by me. Even now, though it is the attractive force behind all my immediate aims, my essential aim is hard to describe precisely because I live it rather than choose it. Yet if all my immediate aims are chosen in view of my essential aim, should they not in some way point to it? Can they not tell me about my essential aim itself, about what it is that my heart has followed all my days but cannot name?

Perhaps it is easier to begin by considering what my essential aim is not. Thinking back to Aristotle again, I have to agree with him that it cannot consist in material pleasures. For however intense they might be, they are ultimately unsatisfying if for no other reason than that they are passing, fleeting, like water running through my fingers. Yet what I really desire is to lay hold of value that I can keep without losing it.

Aristotle says the same thing about reputation and a sense of power. They too are ephemeral. What better examples of this than Alcibiades or the young man Aristotle is reputed to have tutored in his youth? Alexander did live a dazzling life but for how long?

Well, what about interpersonal relationships? Do they not constitute the best sort of experience? Yes, this seems highly probable, though I also note sadly that even those whom I love do die and are taken out of my life. Interpersonal relationships themselves are haunted by fragility and incompleteness.

I try another tack. The Oracle's admonition is directed toward knowing, understanding. Do I not have a natural appetite for that? And would not knowing myself include knowing my relationships both to the world around me and to the people I encounter?

I do in fact find that my thirst for knowledge is open-ended. Of course the limitations of my own personality place unfortunate limits on my interests, yet in general I find that I would like to know not only about this or that sort of being, but about beings of all sorts, or even the understructure of being—which is to say, metaphysical philosophy. There is more I desire to know than I shall ever have time to learn.

With these initial observations I can focus more exactly on the problem of knowing myself. I find it convenient to frame this search as follows.

These are stated as nonexclusive of one another and in no special order:

(a) I am free to utilize the metaphysical perspective that I have adopted in the previous development.

(b) What I am and what I do is primarily inspired by my essential aim; it is a drive toward self-fulfillment, and hence it is the key to knowing myself.

(c) My essential aim is *given* me by Alpha and is a life-long ideal.

(d) All my immediate aims participate in my essential aim as contributing to it.

(e) My essential aim is tailored by Alpha according to the universal pattern of possibility and according to the limits of my world situation and my particular biological inheritance.

(f) My essential aim governs my essential character and consequently my capabilities for activity.

(g) My drive toward an aim is an instance of the general thrust of the act of existing back toward its source, which is Alpha/Omega. (In section 11.4 I called this the bipolarity of the act of existing.)

(h) I accept the general principle that activities reveal the potentialities that enable them. Roughly, one way of knowing what I am is to look at what I do.

16.3.2 Particular facts of experience

(i) I find myself lured not just to particular goods but, somehow, to the Good. Everything I desire has the aspect of good—and that means richer existing—yet no good that I have ever experienced adequately satisfies this desire. There is always a sense of incompleteness.

(j) In particular, my desire transcends anything material, it goes beyond space and time. Physical enjoyment breeds its own weariness, and in any case it cannot last.

(k) Yet the good that I ultimately desire is a good that in some way I would possess and possess permanently. Only a good that I could never lose would ultimately satisfy my drive.

(l) Yet no matter what such a possessing might consist of, I do not see how it could be permanent. Indeed, any possessing that is permanent seems simply incompatible with human mortality. As Heidegger pointed out, we humans, precisely as such, carry in our psyches the specter of possible nonexistence.

(m) Perhaps Aquinas is right, however, in identifying this possessing with an activity of my intellect by which I grasp the Good Itself insofar as it is given to me.[6]

(n) That my desire transcends materiality, however, is not surprising since my thought clearly does that. Signs of that are: the self-reflexivity of knowing (knowing that I know), and the human ability to grasp universal concepts both as such (even to understanding whole logical or mathematical systems of them) and as instantiated in particular bodies though not *as* universals. I grant that there is an undeniable dependence of my thinking on my brain states, yet it does not follow that thinking is nothing other than brain processes. Logically it may just as well be that the right brain processes are a necessary condition for thinking, not thinking itself, and there are strong reasons for thinking that that is exactly the case.[7]

(o) I have argued above[8] that Alpha adjusts each immediate aim exactly to the situation of the nascent primary being and to what is best possible for it in view of Alpha's knowledge of the universal order of possibility. It would therefore appear paradoxical, if not contradictory, that Alpha should furnish any primary being with an essential aim that is in principle impossible of fulfillment.

16.4 CONCLUSIONS AND LIMIT QUESTIONS

In the end, then, I seem to have achieved some better knowledge of myself. I understand what makes me one even though

I am also complex. My unity lies in my directedness toward my essential aim, an aim that all my parts share in. All my immediate aims and their corresponding activities arise from a drive toward my own self-fulfillment, and this drive is an instance of the universal thrust of the act of existing back toward its source, which is Existing Itself under the aspect of the Good.[9] I also understand better how I relate to the world and the world to me in causal interactivity. My perceived world is the real world, though not the world in itself, and my perception of it and reaction to it is part of what I am. The most meaningful aspect of such interactivity occurs in interpersonal relationships.

Yet I am left with limit questions that philosophy seems unable to answer. On the one hand I find myself drawn to the Good as such, but I never encounter it. I long to possess it, but I don't even know what that would mean and certainly I haven't possessed it yet. And though such possession would be incomplete if it were to be ultimately erased by time, yet my death is inevitable. Death eventually puts an effective end even to interpersonal relationships.

So it seems that my essential aim, which attracts me to the Good, must necessarily be frustrated even though it is given me by Alpha who, to speak humanly, should know better. But perhaps there is some way in which I am to transcend even death itself and possess the Good in a way that I cannot now imagine or conceive. Ideally I should expect this possessing to be some form of interpersonal relationship, if that is conceivable, with Alpha Itself. How could this be possible?

Thus I find myself at the farthest boundary of philosophy, asking questions that philosophy itself, so far as I can see, cannot answer. If there is another horizon beyond where I have gone it does not belong to philosophy, it belongs to religion and theology. And if that is the case, then perhaps that itself is the most important thing about myself that I have discovered in trying to respond to the challenge of the Oracle.

Notes

PREFACE

1. Etienne Gilson, *The Unity of Philosophical Experience*, 248; italics in the original. Here and in all further citations, see the bibliography for complete publication information.

2. James W. Felt, "Invitation to a Philosophic Revolution."

3. The above views have naturally found expression in my published essays and in my books, *Making Sense of Your Freedom* (1984; repr. 2005), *Coming To Be* (2001), and *Human Knowing: A Prelude to Metaphysics* (2005).

4. George Berkeley, *A Treatise Concerning the Principles of Human Knowledge*, 4.

Chapter 1   THE BEGINNING

1. The relation between philosophic and scientific understanding constitutes a rich epistemological topic that will be at least touched on later in this essay.

2. Henri Bergson, *The Creative Mind*, 124.

3. Alfred North Whitehead, *Process and Reality*, 112.

4. This assumption is obviously in need of further refinement, and I shall undertake that later. For the present I propose it as a tentative though reasonable hypothesis.

5. I am not the first to use the phrase "relational realism." To my knowledge it was first used by W. Norris Clarke, though perhaps in a somewhat different sense, in his essay "Action as the Self-Revelation of Being," (in *Explorations in Metaphysics,* 59). In any case, the phrase is exactly apt to express what I mean here. I develop this theory more completely in my essay, "Relational Realism and the Great Deception of Sense," and more fully still in *Human Knowing: A Prelude to Metaphysics.*

6. I shall further develop the point about causality in the next chapter.

Chapter 2 A BRIEF DESCRIPTION OF EXPERIENCING

1. Alfred North Whitehead, who was perhaps the first philosopher explicitly to recognize this aspect of immediate sense experience, called it "perception in the mode of causal efficacy." See his *Process and Reality,* part 2, chap. 8, "Symbolic Reference"; also his *Symbolism,* especially chap. 2.

2. David Hume, *A Treatise of Human Nature,* book 1, part 4, section 6, 252.

3. Reported by William Ernest Hocking in "Whitehead as I Knew Him," 8.

Chapter 3 INTERLUDE ON METHOD

1. It can even be argued, though I shall not do it here, that human consciousness is also one of these factors, so that human sensation belongs to a different horizon from that of other animals.

2. Etienne Gilson, *The Unity of Philosophical Experience,* 243.

3. Aldous Huxley, *Brave New World,* xviii.

4. Were this an essay focused on the philosophy of St. Thomas Aquinas, it would be customary to refer to him as "Thomas" inasmuch as "Aquinas" is not a patronymic but rather a place name. But in the present essay it will be clearer to say "Aquinas," and it may be thought that after more than seven centuries Aquinas has earned the name for himself.

5. W. Norris Clarke, "Analogy and the Meaningfulness of Language about God," 131.

6. The notion of "primary being" will be discussed in section 4.4.

7. Here I explicitly reject the independent existence of anything like Plato's Forms, Whitehead's eternal objects, or Leibniz's and David Lewis's possible worlds.

8. Aristotle says: "It is *not* absurd that the actualization of one thing should be in another. Teaching is the activity of a person who can teach, yet the operation is performed *on* some patient—it is not cut adrift from a subject, but is of *A* on *B*"; *Physics,* book 3, chap. 3, 202b5; in *The Basic Works of Aristotle,* 257.

9. See Whitehead's *Process and Reality,* part 2, chap. 8, "Symbolic Reference."

10. This assumption is shared by both Aquinas and Whitehead, though each in his own way.

11. The notion "primary being" will be elucidated in the following chapter, section 4.4.

12. The reader familiar with Whitehead will recognize that I am here controverting his conception of the genesis of an "actual entity," in which the feeler of the feelings originating the actual entity is in a technical but strong sense more derivative from the feelings than presupposed by them. Roughly, the feelings are given ontologically prior to the feeler which ultimately arises out of them. But Whitehead adopted this view largely in order to avoid making his ultimate units into "substances," which he understood in the senses of Descartes, Locke, and Hume, and which he understandably but erroneously read back into the text of Aristotle. This had in my view far-reaching and regrettable consequences for contemporary process philosophy. I have made this argument in some detail in my essay, "Whitehead's Misconception of 'Substance' in Aristotle."

Chapter 4   A PRELIMINARY METAPHYSICAL INTERPRETATION
            OF EXPERIENCE

1. Although I have accepted, with Whitehead, the authenticity of this feeling of derivation of present experience from the past, I here radically part from him in interpreting its metaphysical structure. For complex reasons of his own Whitehead could not allow that his metaphysical ultimates (his "actual entities") are intrinsically temporal, nor that a human person, for example, is a single actual entity perduring through time rather than a serial succession of entities each

of which realizes a minute thickness of time but none of which is internally temporal.

2. Peter Bertocci has made this case against the Whiteheadian position in his essay, "Hartshorne and Personal Identity: A Personalistic Critique."

3. Aristotle, *Metaphysics,* book 7 (Zeta), chap. 1, 1028b2–4.

4. See Edward Pols's discussion of this usage in his *Acts of Our Being,* 196.

Chapter 5 AIMS AND THE EXPERIENCING SUBJECT

1. I am endeavoring here to correct the position I erroneously took in *Coming To Be,* especially pages 84–88, where I attributed individuation to subjective aim rather than to bodily differentiation. There I was, as I see now, confusing the principle of internal self-identity of a primary being with the principle of individuation from others. The former is rightly attributable to aim (or in Thomism to substantial form), but the latter to the nonformal, quantitative limitations of body. However contrived the medieval conception of the latter may seem to us now, it was not meant to define the former.

2. Here and throughout, it will be clear to the reader from the context that I am using "being" as shorthand for "primary being."

Chapter 6 THE OBJECT-STRUCTURE OF IMMEDIATE EXPERIENCE: SPACE

1. See, for instance, Nicholas Rescher, *Leibniz: An Introduction to His Philosophy,* 84–85; and Herbert Wildon Carr, *Leibniz,* 153.

2. One such expression, among many, is in Alfred North Whitehead, *Process and Reality,* 76.

3. The reader familiar with Whitehead will notice that I am here denying his contention that the fundamental entities (his actual entities or actual occasion) do not themselves move.

4. Aristotle, *Physics,* book 4, chap. 11, 219b; in *The Basic Works of Aristotle,* 292.

5. The classic example of this near identity is given by Sir Isaac Newton in the famous Scholium to his *Principia*; see Newton, Mathematical Principles, 1:6.

Chapter 7   THE SUBJECT-STRUCTURE OF IMMEDIATE EXPERIENCE: TIME

1. Here, of course, I am rejecting Whitehead's description of the person as a tightly ordered strand of successive and distinct occasions of experience.

2. Saint Augustine, *Confessions,* book 11, 235.

3. Today we more readily say "in the mind" than "in the soul," but then, as intellectual heirs of Descartes, we only with difficulty avoid his fatal dualism between pure mind and pure bodily extension. Augustine's "soul" was a richer notion than Descartes' "mind."

Chapter 8   ON THE INTERACTIONS OF PRIMARY BEINGS

1. Sir Arthur Eddington, *The Nature of the Physical World,* xi.

2. In the following chapter I shall discuss in more detail this claim of the authenticity of our feeling of freedom.

3. It is to be noticed that the assumption that no information can be communicated in the universe at a rate faster than the speed of light (a tenet now commonly referred to as *locality*) is no longer clearly tenable even scientifically. See the extensive discussion on this in Shimon Malin, *Nature Loves to Hide.*

4. In this way relational realism accounts for the temporal characteristics of sense perception in a more natural way, it seems to me, than does Whitehead's theory of "perception in the mode of presentational immediacy" with his rather convoluted way of relating it to the other "mode of causal efficacy."

5. Notably in Alfred North Whitehead, *Modes of Thought,* lecture 6.

6. See the excellent elaboration of this point in W. Norris Clarke, *Person and Being,* 5–13.

Chapter 9   FREE ACTS

1. This is the conception of freedom accepted, for instance, by John Locke in his *An Essay Concerning Human Understanding,* 1:315 and 1:327, that has, unfortunately for subsequent philosophy, served as the model for most discussions of human freedom.

2. This argument is the theme of my introductory essay, *Making Sense of Your Freedom: Philosophy for the Perplexed.*

3. I have tried to review the main objections against freedom, with their replies, in *Making Sense of Your Freedom.*

4. Locke, *Essay,* 1:317.

5. It would not even be correct to think that the act of deciding simply actualizes some preexistent possibility, since the very determinateness of such a supposed possibility depends upon, and hence cannot precede, the free act. This is what Bergson meant in maintaining that the possible does not precede the real (in *The Creative Mind,* chap. 3, "The Possible and the Real"). To give a satisfactory argument in support of this point would, unfortunately, take us too far afield here. I have made such an argument in my essay, "Why Possible Worlds Aren't."

Chapter 10   THE BASIC STRUCTURE OF PRIMARY BEINGS

1. Once again, one may see my essay, "Whitehead's Misconception of 'Substance' in Aristotle."

2. For instance, in Alfred North Whitehead, *Process and Reality,* 162–64 and 187–88.

3. It has in fact a long history in Whitehead scholarship inasmuch as many scholars have been dissatisfied with his eventual description of the human person in terms of a "personally ordered society" of distinct, successive actual occasions. Some references to this can be found in my *Coming To Be,* 70.

4. A classic text from Aquinas on virtual existence is his *Summa Theologiae,* I , 76, 4 reply 4.

5. As I did in my *Coming To Be,* 70, I prefer to say "subordinate entities" rather than "subordinate beings" to emphasize that although these components are in one sense primary beings in their own right, yet by reason of their participation in the essential aim of the primary being of which they are a part, they are better thought of in this relation of *intrinsic functional dependence* on the complex primary being.

I suggested this view somewhat tentatively in *Coming To Be,* 70–71. I do it here more confidently and in somewhat more detail. Only after arriving at that position did I notice that Terence L. Nichols had proposed a very similar view—what he calls *subsidiarity*—in "Aquinas's Concept of Substantial Form and Modern Science." I am more encouraged than embarrassed by this agreement.

6. The reader will have noticed the affinity between this conception of primary being and that of Leibniz, of Whitehead, and even of Aquinas. The first two comparisons are evident enough, but I call attention to the third. Like Aquinas, I think of the essence of the primary being as a capacity for existential act and existential activities, and I venture to think that my notion of essential character, together with its determining essential aim, performs the function, in Aquinas's view, of substantial form in its formal, effective, and final causality.

Chapter 11 EXISTING AS PARTICIPATED ACT

1. "Warum ist überhaupt Seiendes und nicht vielmehr Nichts?" (my translation). In Martin Heidegger, *Einführung in die Metaphysik*, 1.

2. In a graduate seminar at Saint Louis University under Professor Leo Sweeney, S.J., I found this compellingly demonstrated from our comprehensive survey of Aquinas's writings examined in their chronological order. It also seemed clear, from the shift in Aquinas's expressions, that this perspective gradually grew in strength and clarity in his own mind.

3. I am indebted to Professor William Desmond for pointing out to me, quite rightly, that my earlier book, *Coming To Be,* would more appropriately have been entitled *Becoming* since I was not there principally dealing with this more radical act of coming to be.

4. It should be noticed that the essential dependence of a created universe on its Creator does not require that there have been a beginning in time, only that whenever the universe exists it be in essential dependence on its Creator. Aquinas did not in fact see any purely philosophical argument that proved a beginning in time. He only supposed such a beginning because he understood the book of Genesis to assert it.

5. In section 4.1, I used the phrase "the bipolarity of experiencing" to describe the subject-object or subject-world aspect of the act of experiencing. Here, however, I am once again utilizing the analogy of (existential) bipolarity but to point to something quite different.

6. W. Norris Clarke identifies three essential components of participation in the thought of Aquinas: (1) That the source of the participated "perfection" (here the act of existing) possesses that perfection in an unlimited way; (2) that it be received by the participant in a limited way; and (3) by reason of the causal influence of the source

(in his "The Meaning of Participation in St. Thomas," 94). I think he might well have added a fourth component, the aspect of "existential bipolarity" that I just described.

Chapter 12   PARTICIPATION AND GOD

1. Here I am unabashedly supposing that our experience puts us in touch with an extramental universe, not just with our own impressions of one. Hence we are questioning what is required of the universe itself if it is to be intrinsically intelligible, not just of how we must *think* of a universe.

2. Aquinas, *Summa Theologiae,* I, 2, 3.

3. In this argument I attempt to meld Aquinas's Third Way with Whitehead's "ontological principle" as found variously expressed in his *Process and Reality* (see its index). In what follows I make use of some of Whitehead's less formal expressions of it.

4. Whitehead, *Process and Reality,* 244.

5. Even the Big Bang theory does not go so far as to assert that prior to the Big Bang there was absolutely nothing at all. From the present state of the universe it extrapolates back in time to a singularity from which not only the universe but also space and time themselves evolved. Nothing can be scientifically asked, or answered, concerning any state prior to that singularity.

6. It would not be technically difficult, but is too distracting here for its worth, to show that there could not be more than one such being.

7. G. W. Leibnitz, "On the Ultimate Origination of Things," 42.

Chapter 13   THE PROBLEM OF THE ORIGIN OF ESSENTIAL AIMS

1. In the Scholastic tradition, *esse* is often called the being's "first" (meaning most fundamental) act, and its activity, its *agere,* its "second" act.

2. It is a defect in my previous essay, *Coming To Be,* that I did not keep this distinction clearly in mind.

3. See for instance, Aquinas, *Summa Theologiae,* I, 15, 2.

4. Alfred North Whitehead, *Process and Reality,* 343.

5. Ibid., 244.

6. See especially my *Coming To Be,* 56–59.

1. Some chief texts of Aquinas on the origin of substantial forms are found in his *On the Truth of the Catholic Faith* (the *Summa Contra Gentiles*), book 3, chap. 69: "On the Opinion of Those Who Take Away Proper Actions from Natural Things,"and in the *Summa Theologiae,* I, 90, 2, "Is the soul created?"; 118, 1, "Is the sense-soul transmitted with the semen?"; and 118, 2, "Is the intellectual soul caused from semen?"

2. Aquinas, *On the Truth of the Catholic Faith,* book 3, chaps. 66–69.

3. Aquinas, *Summa Theologiae,* I, 118, 1, c.

4. Once again, one may see my essay, "Whitehead's Misconception of 'Substance' in Aristotle."

5. Alfred North Whitehead, *Process and Reality,* 59, 73, and passim.

6. Whitehead supposes that the orientation of God's primordial nature is always toward enhancement of value experience, but he can at best take this simply as a pure supposition based on our own limited experience. Aquinas can do better, metaphysically speaking, when he identifies Existing Itself with the Good.

7. This is quite explicit in Whitehead (see section 10.9 above) and at least implicit in Aquinas.

8. William Ernest Hocking, "Whitehead as I Knew Him," 15.

1. William James, "The Dilemma of Determinism," 146.

2. In *Coming To Be* I already inclined to this view (see in that Index under "Subjective aim and God"), and I am even more persuaded of it now.

3. Aquinas, *On the Truth of the Catholic Faith,* book 3, chap. 68.

4. The groundwork for this remarkable view of an interactivity between God and the world is sketched—just barely—by Whitehead in the very last part of *Process and Reality,* "God and the World."

5. Insofar as Whitehead deals with existence, he roots it in his principle, Creativity, which is a drive toward constantly synthesizing a given Many of actual entities into a new One. Whitehead however does not think of this drive as flowing from God; God is rather its

primordial instance and gives it its character in determining the value relationships of all the "eternal objects" (patterns of existence). Notice here that Whitehead's system is basically a pluralism of entities seeking unity, whereas Aquinas's begins with a One that freely constitutes a Many through participative creation.

Also, my primary entities are more like Thomistic substances than Whiteheadian actual entities at least in this, that I conceive them to endure through whatever span of time is required for the achievement of their respective essential aims. I thus make a clear distinction between the coming to be of an entity and its own activity. Functionally, therefore, my essential aim plays a somewhat different role than does Whitehead's initial aim. Yet the question as to their origin is approximately the same.

6. As we have already seen, for instance, in Aquinas, *On the Truth of the Catholic Faith,* book 3, chap. 69.

7. In this way Aquinas borrows from and adapts Plotinus's theory of emanation and return.

8. See for instance Aquinas, *On the Truth of the Catholic Faith,* book 3, chap. 70.

9. David Lewis, *On the Plurality of Worlds,* 207.

10. Etienne Gilson, *The Unity of Philosophical Experience,* 243.

11. I give a more careful account in section 5.2 above.

12. W. Norris Clarke, "Review of James W. Felt, *Coming to Be,*" 185.

13. Aquinas, *On the Power of God (Quaestiones Disputatae de Potentia Dei),* question 3, article 7, 124–25. (Compare also the parallel treatment in Aquinas's *On the Truth of the Catholic Faith,* book 3, chap. 67.)

14. Aquinas, *On the Power of God,* 127.

15. Ibid., 132.

16. Aquinas, *Summa theologiae,* I, 118, 1, ad 3.

17. Ibid., 133; emphasis added.

18. Ibid., 134; emphasis added.

19. Aquinas, *On the Truth of the Catholic Faith,* book 3, chap. 69.

20. For the simplest instance of this in Aquinas, see his Second Way for demonstrating God in the *Summa Theologiae,* I, 2, 3.

21. "Ergo est aliquis intelligens a quo omnes res naturales ordinantur ad finem, et hoc dicimus Deum"; Aquinas, *Summa Theologiae,* I, 2, 3 (Blackfriars edition and translation). Some editions write "aliquid" instead of "aliquis."

1. Act I, scene II.

2. E. B. White, "The Door," 288.

3. Aristotle, *Nicomachean Ethics,* book 10, chap. 7.

4. Notice that this is a distinct question from asking the source of my individuation. I did not keep this distinction sufficiently in mind in *Coming To Be.*

5. This holds true, from the standpoint of the theory of participation in the act of existing, regardless of whether one adopts the view, as I did in the preceding chapter, that Alpha furnishes the essential aim not only in the case of the emergence of a higher form of existing but also in the more ordinary case of animal generation.

6. See Aquinas, *Summa Theologiae,* I-II, 2, 8.

7. I have given a cumulative argument for this conclusion in my *Human Knowing: A Prelude to Metaphysics,* passim.

8. In section 15.1 (d).

9. This drive toward the Good would naturally ground an ontology-based ethics.

Bibliography

Aquinas, St. Thomas. *On the Power of God (Quaestiones Disputatae de Potentia Dei)*. Trans. the English Dominican Fathers. Westminster, Maryland: The Newman Press, 1952.

————. *On the Truth of the Catholic Faith (Summa Contra Gentiles)*. Book Three: *Providence,* Part 1. Trans., with Introduction and Notes, Vernon J. Bourke. Garden City, New York: 1956.

————. *Summa Theologiae*. Blackfriars ed. New York: McGraw Hill Book Company, 1964.

Aristotle. *The Basic Works of Aristotle*. Ed. Richard McKeon. New York: Random House, 1941.

————. *Metaphysics*. Trans. Richard Hope. Ann Arbor: University of Michigan Press, 1960.

Augustine, Saint. *Confessions*. Trans. Henry Chadwick. Oxford: Oxford University Press, 1992.

Bergson, Henri. *The Creative Mind*. Totowa, New Jersey: Littlefield, Adams & Co., 1975.

Berkeley, George. *A Treatise Concerning the Principles of Human Knowledge*. New York: Liberal Arts Press, 1957.

Bertocci, Peter. "Hartshorne and Personal Identity: A Personalistic Critique." *Process Studies* 2 (Fall 1972): 216–21.

Carr, Herbert Wildon. *Leibniz*. New York: Dover Publications, 1960.

Clarke, W. Norris, S.J. "Action as the Self-Revelation of Being: A Central Theme in the Thought of St. Thomas," In *History of Philosophy in the Making,* ed. Linus J. Thro, S.J. Washington, D.C.:

University Press of America, 1982; repr. in Clarke, *Explorations in Metaphysics.*

———. "Analogy and the Meaningfulness of Language about God." In Clarke, *Explorations in Metaphysics.*

———. *Explorations in Metaphysics: Being—God—Person.* Notre Dame, Indiana: University of Notre Dame Press, 1994.

———. "The Meaning of Participation in St. Thomas." In Clarke, *Explorations in Metaphysics.*

———. *Person and Being.* Milwaukee: Marquette University Press, 1993.

———. "Review of James W. Felt, *Coming To Be.*" *Process Studies* 31 (Spring–Summer 2002): 183–85.

Eddington, Sir Arthur. *The Nature of the Physical World.* Ann Arbor: University of Michigan Press, 1963.

Felt, James W. *Coming To Be: Toward a Thomistic-Whiteheadian Metaphysics of Becoming.* Albany: State University of New York Press, 2001.

———. *Human Knowing: A Prelude to Metaphysics.* Notre Dame, Indiana: University of Notre Dame Press, 2005.

———. "Invitation to a Philosophic Revolution." *The New Scholasticism* 45 (Winter 1971): 87–109.

———. *Making Sense of Your Freedom: Philosophy for the Perplexed.* Ithaca, New York: Cornell University Press; repr. Notre Dame, Indiana: University of Notre Dame Press, 2005.

———. "Relational Realism and the Great Deception of Sense." *The Modern Schoolman* 71 (1994): 305–16.

———. "Whitehead's Misconception of 'Substance' in Aristotle." *Process Studies* 14 (Winter 1985): 224–36.

———. "Why Possible Worlds Aren't." *The Review of Metaphysics* 50 (September 1996): 63–77.

Ford, Lewis S. "Physical Purpose and the Origination of the Subjective Aim." *Process Studies* 31 (Spring–Summer 2004): 71–79.

Gilson, Etienne. *The Unity of Philosophical Experience.* San Francisco: Ignatius Press, 1999.

Heidegger, Martin. *Being and Time.* Trans. John Macquarrie and Edward Robinson. New York: Harper & Row, 1962.

———. *Einführung in die Metaphysik.* Tübingen: Max Niemeyer Verlag, 1966.

———. *An Introduction to Metaphysics.* Trans. Ralph Manheim. Garden City, New York: Anchor Books, 1961.

Hocking, William Ernest. "Whitehead as I Knew Him." In Kline, *Alfred North Whitehead*, 7–17.

Hume, David. *A Treatise of Human Nature*. Ed. L. A. Selby-Bigge. Oxford: Clarendon Press, 1968.

Huxley, Aldous. *Brave New World*. New York: Harper, 1946.

James, William. "The Dilemma of Determinism." In *The Will to Believe, and Other Essays in Popular Philosophy; and Human Immortality: Two Supposed Objections to the Doctrine*, 145–83. New York: Dover Publications, 1956.

Kline, George L., ed. *Alfred North Whitehead: Essays on His Philosophy.* Englewood Cliffs, New Jersey: Prentice-Hall, Inc., 1963.

Kuhn, Thomas S., *The Structure of Scientific Revolutions*. 3rd ed. Chicago: University of Chicago Press, 1996.

Leclerc, Ivor. *The Nature of Physical Existence*. New York: Humanities Press, 1972.

Leibniz, G. W. "On the Ultimate Origination of Things." In *Discourse on Metaphysics and Other Essays*, 41–48. Indianapolis: Hackett Publishing Co., 1991.

Lewis, David. *On the Plurality of Worlds*. New York: Basil Blackwell, 1986.

Locke, John. *An Essay Concerning Human Understanding*. 2 vols. New York: Dover Publications, 1959.

Malin, Shimon. *Nature Loves to Hide: Quantum Physics and Reality, A Western Perspective*. New York: Oxford University Press, 2001.

Newton, Sir Isaac. *Mathematical Principles of Natural Philosophy and His System of the World*. 2 vols. Trans. Andrew Motte, rev. Florian Cajori. Berkeley: University of California Press, 1962.

Nichols, Terence L. "Aquinas's Concept of Substantial Form and Modern Science." *International Philosophical Quarterly* 36 (September 1996): 303–18.

Pols, Edward. *The Acts of Our Being: A Reflection on Agency and Responsibility*. Amherst: University of Massachusetts Press, 1982.

Rescher, Nicholas. *Leibniz: An Introduction to His Philosophy*. Totowa, New Jersey: Rowman and Littlefield, 1979.

———. "The Promise of Process Philosophy." In *Process Philosophy: A Survey of Basic Issues*, 3–21. (Pittsburgh: University of Pittsburgh Press, 2000).

White, E. B., "The Door." In *50 Great Short Stories* ed. Milton Crane, 286–90. New York: Bantam Books, 1971.

Whitehead, Alfred North. *Modes of Thought.* New York: The Free Press, 1968.

———. *Process and Reality,* corrected edition. New York: The Free Press, 1978.

———. *Symbolism, Its Meaning and Effect.* New York: Macmillan, 1927.

Index

act of existing, xi, 20; and
bipolarity, 103; concep-
tually invisible, 21; and
human experience, 20, 63,
120; and potentiality, 21;
structure of, 61, 120
actual entity: its genesis in
Whitehead, 129n12;
and motion, 130n3
(chap. 6)
actuality and possibility, 21–22
agency: and experience, 25,
27, 55–56; and freedom,
59–60
aims: description of, 25; and
existence, 24; participation
of aims, 68–69; and the
universe, 64; and value,
24. *See also* essential aims;
immediate aims
Alpha: as Alpha/Omega, 86,
94; and the bipolarity of
existing, 101, 108; as
furnishing the act of

existing, 101, 103, 107,
121, 124; and God, 78;
as origin of aims, 87, 91,
94, 100–101, 108, 112,
121, 124; as source of
existing and value, 24, 78,
81, 85
animal generation, 90, 95, 102
appearance and reality, 4–5
Aquinas, Saint Thomas: on the
causal activity of heavenly
bodies, 111; on existing
as the ground of value,
28, 61, 121; and the "Five
Ways," 78; on the human
drive toward God, 124; on
participation of existing,
xi, 71–75, 77–78; on
substantial form, 84,
89–90; on teleology, 36,
129n10; and "Thomas,"
128n4; on unitary beings,
67; on the universal order
of possibility, 86

Aristotle: on cause and effect, 22, 46, 50, 129n8; on primary beings, 30, 61, 84; on ultimate aim, happiness, 19–22, 121; on unitary beings, 67

Augustine, Saint, on time, 42

becoming, "horizontal" dimension, 72; "vertical" dimension, coming to be, 72

beings. *See* primary beings

Bergson, Henri, xi, 3, 30; on the possible and the real, 132n5 (chap. 9)

Berkeley, George, xi

Big Bang theory, 134n5 (chap. 12)

bipolarity: of the act of existing, 75–76, 86, 94, 103, 133n5; in experience of subject-object, 13, 27–28

causal efficacy (Whitehead), 27

causal influence, 10, 119

causes: Aristotle on cause and effect, 22; effective (efficient) and final, 22, 24, 58, 94, 102–3; feeling of causal influence, 22, 46; and origination, 58

Clarke, W. Norris, S. J., xii, 108–10, 113, 128n5 (chap. 1); on participation of existing, 133n6 (chap. 11); review of *Coming To Be*, 108

consciousness, 3

continuity: of object-time, 40; of space, 39–40, 130n5; of subject-time, 43

cosmic process, 6–7

cosmological argument for God, from participation of existing, 77–79

creation, as a unique act, 74–75, 133n4

Creativity, Whitehead's Principle of, 135n5 (chap. 15)

Darwinian natural selection, 85

deism, 113

derivation: and causal connectedness, 29; experience of, 10, 63, 119; of present from past, 129n1; and temporal structure, 29

Descartes, René: and appearance and reality, 5; on metaphysical method, 118; on space, 39

Desmond, William, on "coming to be" and "becoming," 133n3

Eddington, Arthur, 47–48

Einstein, Albert, on simultaneity, 49

essential aims: and Alpha, 102–3; description of, 32, 62; feeling of, 12, 22, 64, 105; and freedom, 33; and initial aims (Whitehead), 93; origin of, 83–88, 96, 107; relation to essential character, 32; relation to formal and final causality, 33; relation to the world, 48–49; requirements for, 85, 104; as self-ideals, 119;

AIMS

|

144

and subjective aims
(Whitehead), 87, 94; and
substantial form (Aquinas),
89; and the unity of a
complex being, 67–68,
120, 133n6 (chap. 10)
essential character: description
of, 32, 62; relation to
essential aim, 32, 62,
133n6 (chap. 10)
eternal objects (Whitehead),
129n7
existing, act of: as actualizing
potentiality, 32; and
essential character, 32; as
participated act, 71–76;
and time, 32
experience: and act of existing,
21, 25, 63; as bipolar, 25,
27–28; and objects, 9–10,
120; and possibility,
63–64; of self-identity over
time, 67; and structure of
all beings, 30; of value, 28

"Five Ways" of Aquinas, 78,
115, 136n20
form of definiteness, 63
freedom, 55–60; and agency,
55, 59–60; in all activity
as goal-oriented, 64; causal
arguments against, 57–59;
external and internal,
55–56; in nature, 60, 114;
not demonstrable or
refutable, 56

Gilson, Etienne: on nature
of metaphysics, ix; on
philosophic principles,
19, 104

goal-directedness: of experiencing, 44; in nature,
22–25, 64. *See also*
teleology
God: as active in nature, 90,
100; and Alpha, 78; and
goal-orientation of entities,
108–9; and participation,
74, 77–81; as source of
existing, 107
Gold, Thomas, on choosing
hypotheses, 99

Heidegger, Martin, 61, 71, 124
horizons and perspectives, x,
17–19
human beings: as acting, 55;
as single primary beings
over a lifetime, 129n1,
84; Whitehead on, 93,
131n1 (chap. 7), 132n3
(chap. 10)
human relationships, 52–53
Hume, David: on causality 10,
46, 50; on the experience
of self, 13–14
Huxley, Aldous, 19
hylomorphism, 89–90, 101,
109, 113

immediate aims, 36, 64–65,
84, 121
immediate experience, 3,
117–20
individuation: ground of,
34–35, 120, 130n1
(chap. 5); and personal
unity, 120; problem of,
31, 33–35; retraction of
author's previous position,
130n1 (chap. 5)

interpersonal relationships,
52–53, 119–20, 122,
125; Whitehead on
intersubjectivity, 15

James, William, on adopting
philosophic positions, 99

Kant, Immanuel, and the
world, 38–39

Leibniz, G.W.: and an
argument for God, 80;
on space, 39
Lewis, David, on philosophic
positions, 104
life-span of a primary being,
121
Locke, John: on appearance
and reality, 5; on freedom,
131n1 (chap. 9); on
human experience and
metaphysics, 3

Malin, Shimon, 131n3 (chap. 8)
meaning, sense of, as grounded
in aims, 44
mechanism, 114
Merleau-Ponty, Maurice, xi
metaphysics: and adoption
of its principles, 117;
description and function
of, ix–xi; and perspectives,
19–20, 122
mind and matter, 1, 5

necessary being, meaning of, 81
Newton, Isaac, 130n5
Nichols, Terence L., 132n5
(chap. 10)
novelty in the world, 66, 88

occasionalism, 95, 112–13
the One and the Many, 67; in
Aquinas and Whitehead,
135n5 (chap. 15)
ontological principle, 22; and
novel essential sims, 96,
105; and the universal
order of possibility, 94;
of Whitehead, 79, 84–85
origination and the free act,
agency, 56, 58–59

participation: of the act of
existing, xi, 71–76; of
causal power, 113; of
essential aim in immediate
aims, 68–69, 133n6
(chap. 10); and God,
77–81, 101, 105; and
teleology, 76
personal unity, 67–68, 120; as
dynamic and goal-aimed,
120
perspectives: and horizons, x,
17–19, 47; metaphysical,
19–20; and relational
realism, 47; of science
and philosophy, 45–47
phenomenological descriptions,
xi, 118
Plato, on participation 73
Plotinus, xi; and the bipolarity
of existing, 75; on
emanation and return, 73
Pols, Edward, 130n4 (chap. 4)
possibility: and actuality, 12;
essential aims and
immediate aims, 65;
experience of, 63–64;
locus of possibilities,
65–66

About the Author

James W. Felt, S.J., is Professor Emeritus of Philosophy at Santa Clara University. His previous books are *Making Sense of Your Freedom: Philosophy for the Perplexed* (Cornell University Press, 1994; reprinted by University of Notre Dame Press, 2005); *Coming To Be: Toward a Thomistic-Whiteheadian Metaphysics of Becoming* (State University of New York Press, 2001); and *Human Knowing: A Prelude to Metaphysics* (University of Notre Dame Press, 2005). His email address is jfelt@scu.edu.

AIMS

Lightning Source UK Ltd.
Milton Keynes UK
UKHW021849170123
415517UK00012B/1579